Michael M. Dediu

Vivaldi, Bach, Mozart, and Verdi

A chronological and photographic documentary

DERC Publishing House
Tewksbury (Boston), Massachusetts, U. S. A.

Copyright ©2018 by Michael M. Dediu

All rights reserved

Published and printed in the
United States of America
On the Great Seal of the United States are included:
E Pluribus Unum (Out of many, one)
Annuit Coeptis (He has approved of the undertakings)
Novus Ordo Seclorum (New order of the ages)

Library of Congress Control Number: 2018905818

Dediu, Michael M.

Vivaldi, Bach, Mozart, and Verdi
A chronological and photographic documentary

ISBN-13: 978-1-939757-68-5

Preface

"Without music, life would be a mistake" said a great philosopher. This, and the famous quote of Aristotle (384 BC – 322 BC) - "Everybody, by nature, desires knowledge", are so lovely, that I had to write this book, which is focused on four great composers: Antonio Vivaldi (one of the greatest Baroque composers, with over 650 compositions, his best-known work is a series of violin concertos known as "Le Quattro stagioni" ("The Four Seasons")), Johann Sebastian Bach (generally regarded as one of the greatest composers of all time, and also one of the greatest fathers, with 20 children.), Wolfgang Amadeus Mozart (composed more than 600 works, many acknowledged as pinnacles of symphonic, concertante, chamber, operatic, and choral music, he is among the most enduringly popular of classical composers), and Giuseppe Verdi (in his 30s, he had become one of the pre-eminent opera composers in history, and his operas are the most popular today).

Using a chronological order (which gives the correct perspective of events and personalities at any given time, because the time determines everything), this book has a variety of relevant information not only about them, but also about numerous other personalities and important events. There are also over 100 attractive and historic photographs, which add another visual dimension. The more you read, the more you'll love it!

This book brings a rainbow of practical information, from many places and personalities, and all this information will certainly enhance everybody's joie de vivre. I want to thank my wife Sophia for her photo assistance.

These composers are part of our culture, and any reader, from everywhere, will definitely find, in this book of general interest, plenty of useful information, which will help them to better understand our history, and prepare them for a better future.

Michael M. Dediu, Ph. D.

Tewksbury (Boston), U. S. A., 25 May 2018

Italy, Venezia - This Servizio Gondole (Gondole Service) is situated at the south end of La Piazzetta, the south part of Piazza San Marco. In the center back, Isola San Giorgio Maggiore can be seen, with la Chiesa di San Giorgio Maggiore and its Campanile. On the right back, the east end of the island of Giudecca can be seen. For nine centuries the gondole were the main means of transportation and most common watercraft within Venice.

Michael M. Dediu is also the author of these books (which can be found on Amazon.com):

1. Aphorisms and quotations – with examples and explanations
2. Axioms, aphorisms and quotations – with examples and explanations
3. 100 Great Personalities and their Quotations
4. Professor Petre P. Teodorescu – A Great Mathematician and Engineer
5. Professor Ioan Goia – A Dedicated Engineering Professor
6. Venice (Venezia) – a new perspective. A short presentation with photographs
7. La Serenissima (Venice) - a new photographic perspective. A short presentation with many photos
8. Grand Canal – Venice. A new photographic viewpoint. A short presentation with many photos
9. Piazza San Marco – Venice. A different photographic view. A short presentation with many photos
10. Roma (Rome) - La Città Eterna. A new photographic view. A short presentation with many photos
11. Why is Rome so Fascinating? A short presentation with many photos
12. Rome, Boston and Helsinki. A short photographic presentation
13. Rome and Tokyo – two captivating cities. A short photographic presentation
14. Beautiful Places on Earth – A new photographic presentation
15. From Niagara Falls to Mount Fuji via Rome - A novel photographic presentation
16. From the USA and Canada to Italy and Japan - A fresh photographic presentation
17. Paris – Why So Many Call This City Mon Amour - A lovely photographic presentation
18. The City of Light – Paris (La Ville-Lumière) - A kaleidoscopic photographic presentation
19. Paris (Lutetia Parisiorum) – the romance capital of the world - A kaleidoscopic photographic view
20. Paris and Tokyo – a joyful photographic presentation. With a preamble about the Universe

21. From USA to Japan via Canada – A cheerful photographic documentary
22. 200 Wonderful Places, In The Last 50 Years – A personal photographic documentary
23. Must see places in USA and Japan - A kaleidoscopic photographic documentary
24. Grandeurs of the World - A kaleidoscopic photographic documentary
25. Corneliu Leu – writer on the same wavelength as Mark Twain. An American viewpoint
26. From Berkeley to Pompeii via Rome – A kaleidoscopic photographic documentary
27. From America to Europe via Japan - A kaleidoscopic photographic documentary
28. Discover America and Japan - A photographic documentary
29. J. R. Lucas – philosopher on a creative parallel with Plato, An American viewpoint
30. From America to Switzerland via France - A photographic documentary
31. From Bretton Woods to New York via Cape Cod - A photographic documentary
32. Splendid Places on the Atlantic Coast of the U. S. A. - A photographic documentary
33. Fourteen nice Cities on three Continents - A photographic documentary
34. 17 Picturesque Cities on the World Map - A photographic documentary
35. Unforgettable Places from Four Continents including Trump buildings - A photographic documentary
36. Dediu Newsletter, Volume 1, Number 1, 6 December 2016 – Monthly news, review, comments and suggestions for a better and wiser world
37. Dediu Newsletter, Volume 1, Number 2, 6 January 2017 (available at www.derc.com).
38. Dediu Newsletter, Volume 1, Number 3, 6 February 2017 (available at www.derc.com).
39. London and Greenwich, A photographic documentary
40. Dediu Newsletter, Volume 1, Number 4, 6 March 2017 (available also at www.derc.com).

41. Dediu Newsletter, Volume 1, Number 5, 6 April 2017 (available also at www.derc.com).
42. Dediu Newsletter, Volume 1, Number 6, 6 May 2017 (available also at www.derc.com).
43. Dediu Newsletter, Volume 1, Number 7, 6 June 2017 (available also at www.derc.com).
44. London, Oxford and Cambridge, A photographic documentary
45. Dediu Newsletter, Volume 1, Number 8, 6 July 2017 (available also at www.derc.com).
46. Dediu Newsletter, Volume 1, Number 9, 6 August 2017 (available also at www.derc.com).
47. Dediu Newsletter, Volume 1, Number 10, 6 September 2017 (available also at www.derc.com).
48. Three Great Professors: President Woodrow Wilson, Historian Germán Arciniegas, Mathematician Gheorghe Vrănceanu, A chronological and photographic documentary
49. Dediu Newsletter, Volume 1, Number 11, 6 October 2017 (available also at www.derc.com).
50 Dediu Newsletter, Volume 1, Number 12, 6 November 2017 (available also at www.derc.com).
51 Dediu Newsletter, Volume 2, Number 1 (13), 6 December 2017 (available also at www.derc.com).
52 Two Great Leaders: Augustus and George Washington, A chronological and photographic documentary
53. Dediu Newsletter, Volume 2, Number 2 (14), 6 January 2018 (available also at www.derc.com).
54. Newton, Benjamin Franklin, and Gauss, A chronological and photographic documentary
55. Dediu Newsletter, Volume 2, Number 3 (15), 6 February 2018 (available also at www.derc.com).
56. 2017: World Top Events, But Many Little Known, A chronological and photographic documentary
57. Dediu Newsletter, Volume 2, Number 4 (16), 6 March 2018 (available also at www.derc.com).
58. Vergilius, Horatius, Ovidius, and Shakespeare, A chronological and photographic documentary.
59. Dediu Newsletter, Volume 2, Number 5 (17), 6 April 2018 (available also at www.derc.com).

60. Dediu Newsletter, Volume 2, Number 6 (18), 6 May 2018 (available also at www.derc.com).

Italy, Roma - Arco di Costantino (312, left), and Amphitheatrum Flavium (Colosseum, 80 AD, right), from Via di San Gregorio.

Michael M. Dediu is the editor of these books (also on Amazon.com):

1. Sophia Dediu: The life and its torrents – Ana. In Europe around 1920
2. Proceedings of the 4th International Conference "Advanced Composite Materials Engineering" COMAT 2012
3. Adolf Shvedchikov: I am an eternal child of spring – poems in English, Italian, French, German, Spanish and Russian
4. Adolf Shvedchikov: Life's Enigma – poems in English, Italian and Russian
5. Adolf Shvedchikov: Everyone wants to be HAPPY – poems in English, Spanish and Russian
6. Adolf Shvedchikov: My Life, My Love – poems in English, Italian and Russian
7. Adolf Shvedchikov: I am the gardener of love – poems in English and Russian
8. Adolf Shvedchikov: Amaretta di Saronno – poems in English and Russian
9. Adolf Shvedchikov: A Russian Rediscovers America
10. Adolf Shvedchikov: Parade of Life - poems in English and Russian
11. Adolf Shvedchikov: Overcoming Sorrow - poems in English and Russian
12. Sophia Dediu: Sophia meets Japan
13. Corneliu Leu: Roosevelt, Churchill, Stalin and Hitler: Their surprising role in Eastern Europe in 1944
14. Proceedings of the 5th International Conference "Computational Mechanics and Virtual Engineering" COMEC 2013
15. Georgeta Simion – Potanga: Beyond Imagination: A Thought-provoking novel inspired from mid-20th century events
16. Ana Dediu: The poetry of my life in Europe and The USA
17. Ana Dediu: The Four Graces
18. Proceedings of the 5th International Conference "Advanced Composite Materials Engineering" COMAT 2014
19. Sophia Dediu: Chocolate Cook Book: Is there such a thing as too much chocolate?

20. Sorin Vlase: Mechanical Identifiability in Automotive Engineering
21. Gabriel Dima: The Evolution of the Aerostructures – Concept and Technologies
22. Proceedings of the 6th International Conference "Computational Mechanics and Virtual Engineering" COMEC 2015
23. Sophia Dediu: Cook Book 1 A-B-C Common sense cooking
24. Sophia Dediu: Dim Sum Spring Festival
25. Ana Dediu and Sophia Dediu: Europe in 1985: A chronological and photographic documentary

Paris (250 BC): l'Hôtel de Ville (City Hall since 1357, King Francis I started this building in 1533, finished 1628, 1873-1892

Table of Contents

Preface 3

Table of Contents 11

Chapter 1. Antonio Vivaldi and J. C. Bach 13

Chapter 2. Wolfgang Amadeus Mozart 68

Chapter 3. Giuseppe Verdi 94

London, from the Shard (2012, 309 m, observatory at 244 m), looking east to the Tower Bridge (1886-1894, combined bascule and suspension turreted bridge over River Thames (flowing from west (left) to east (right)), between London boroughs Tower Hamlets (north – left up) and Southward (south – right), length 244 m, height 65 m, longest span 82 m, clearance 8 m (closed), 42 m (open)), City Hall (2002, height 45 m, center right round, for the Greater London Authority: Mayor of London and the London Assembly).

Chapter 1. Antonio Vivaldi and J. C. Bach

1678 – 4 March – Antonio Lucio Vivaldi was born in Venezia (Venice, situated on 120 islands formed by 177 canals in the lagoon between the mouths of the Po and Piave rivers, at the northwestern extremity of the Adriatic Sea - became known as the "Queen of the Adriatic" reflecting its historic role as a naval power and commercial center), then the capital of the Republic of Venice (the strongest European power in the Mediterranean region; Venice acquired neighboring territories, and by the late 15th century, the city-state was the leading maritime power in the Christian world). He was baptized immediately after his birth, at his mother home, by the midwife, maybe because of his poor health, or because of an earthquake that shook the city that day.

4 May – Antonio Vivaldi's official church baptism, at San Giovanni in Bragora, Sestiere di Castello, Venezia.

Antonio's parents were Giovanni Battista Vivaldi and Camilla Calicchio, as recorded in the register of San Giovanni in Bragora. Antonio had eight younger siblings: Iseppo Santo Vivaldi, Iseppo Gaetano Vivaldi, Bonaventura Tomaso Vivaldi, Margarita Gabriela Vivaldi, Cecilia Maria Vivaldi, Gerolama Michela Vivaldi, Francesco Gaetano Vivaldi, and Zanetta Anna Vivaldi.

Antonio's father, Giovanni Battista, who was a barber before becoming a professional violinist, taught Antonio to play the violin, and then toured Venezia playing the violin with his young son.

Giovanni Battista, under the name Rossi, was one of the founders of the *Sovvegno dei musicisti di Santa Cecilia*, an association of musicians from Venezia. The president of the *Sovvegno* was Giovanni Legrenzi (12 August 1626 – 27 May 1690, aged 63.7), an early Baroque composer and the *maestro di cappella* at St Mark's Basilica.

The Doge of Venezia was Alvise Contarini, 76.5, (24 October 1601 – 15 January 1684, aged 82.2, the 106th Doge of Venice, reigning from his election on 26 August 1676 (74.8) until his death seven and an almost half years later. He was the eighth and final member of the House of Contarini to serve as Doge of Venice (with the first being Domenico I Contarini, who became Doge in 1043, 633 years earlier).

Tomaso Albinoni was 7 years old (8 June 1671, in Venezia – 17 January 1751, aged 79.5), and he was an older contemporaneous Italian Baroque composer with Vivaldi.

Antonio Stradivari was 34 years old (1644 – 1737, aged 93), already famous in Cremona (60 km west of Virgilio (birthpace of the great Latin poet Vergilius, 15 Oct 70 BC – 21 Sep 19 BC, aged 50.9), 75 km southeast of Milano), north of river Po, in Lombardia, where Stradivari crafted for 81 years (from the age of 12 to 93) the best over 700 violins, cellos, guitars and harps, cold Stradivarius. The first violin was ordered by a descendent of Lorenzo de' Medici (1 Jan 1449 – 8 April 1492, aged 43.2) in 1555, in a letter to Andrea Amati, 50, (c 1505 – c. 1578, aged c. 73), who was the first from the Amati family of luthiers, followed by Antonio and brother Girolamo, Niccolo, and Girolamo (Hieronymus II, 26 Feb 1649 - 21 Feb 1740, aged 5 days before 91).

Italy, Venezia - Piazza San Marco with Palazzo Ducale (right), Libreria Sansoviniana (next to Palazzo Ducale), Basilica di San Marco (back), Giardini Reali and Il Campanile (center-right), Procuratie Nuove (center to left), Capitano di Porto (left).

1681 – 24 March – Vivaldi was 3 years old when Georg Philipp Telemann was born (24 March 1681 – 25 June 1767, aged 86 years 3 months and 1 day, German Baroque composer and multi-instrumentalist)

1684 – 15 January - Antonio was 5.8 years old when the 106th Doge Alvise Contarini died at 82.2.

26 January - Marcantonio Giustinian, 64.9, (March 2, 1619 – March 23, 1688, aged 69 and 21 days) was elected the 107th Doge of Venice, reigning 4.1 years, until his death.

Italy, Venezia - The south façade of Basilica Cattedrale Patriarcale di San Marco, with three of the five domes visible up right.

1685 – Antonio was 7 years old when his father, Giovanni Battista, was admitted as a violinist to the orchestra of the San Marco Basilica in Venice. Antonio learned violin and music theory from his father.

5 March - George Frideric Handel was born in Halle-upon-Saale (5 March 1685 – 14 April 1759, aged 74.1, burial place Westminster Abbey, London).

London - The west façade and entrance of Westminster Abbey (960, 1517, Collegiate Church of St Peter at Westminster, Anglican abbey with daily services and coronations since 1066, tower height 69 m).

31 March – Johann Sebastian Bach was born in Eisenach (31 March 1685 – 28 July 1750, aged 65 years, 3 months and 28 days, in Leipzig). The Bach family already counted several composers when Johann Sebastian was born as the last of the 8 children of a city musician in Eisenach, in the duchy of Saxe-Eisenach, 650 km northwest of Venezia, and 275 km southwest of Berlin. His father, Johann Ambrosius Bach, 40, (22 Feb 1645 – 2 March 1695, aged 50), was the director of the town musicians, and all of his uncles were professional musicians. His father probably taught him to play the violin and harpsichord, and his brother Johann Christoph Bach taught him the clavichord and exposed him to much contemporary music. JSB's mother was Maria Elisabeth Lämmerhirt, 41, (24 Feb 1644 – 1 May 1694, aged 50.2). On 1 April 1668 she married the father (he was 23, and she was 24), and they had eight children, four of whom became musicians, including Johann Sebastian.

1 October - Holy Roman (Austrian) Emperor Charles VI was born.

26 October - Domenico Scarlatti was born in Napoli, (26 Oct 1685 – 23 July 1757, aged 71.7), son of Alessandro Scarlatti (2 May 1660 – 22 Oct 1725, aged 65.4). Handel, Bach and Domenico Scarlatti were contemporaneous: Handel was 26 days older than Bach, and Bach was 6 months and 1 day older than D. Scarlatti, but D. Scarlatti died 6 years, 11 months and 25 days after Bach, and Handel died 1 year, 8 months and 22 days after Domenico Scarlatti.

1687 – 5 Dec – Antonio was 9 when Francesco Saverio Geminiani was born in Lucca (5 Dec 1687 – 17 Sep 1762, Dublin, Ireland, aged 74.8, an Italian violinist, composer, and music theorist; he received lessons in music from Alessandro Scarlatti, 27, (2 May 1660 – 22 Oct 1725, aged 65.4)).

1688 – 23 March – Antonio was 10 when the 107th Doge Marcantonio Giustinian died (March 2, 1619 – March 23, 1688, aged 69 and 21 days).
The 108th Doge was Francesco Morosini, 69, (26 February 1619 – 16 January 1694, aged 74.9), for almost 6 years.

1689 – Antonio, 11, received his first lessons in composition from Giovanni Legrenzi, 62.8.
Antonio's father probably composed an opera titled *La Fedeltà sfortunata*, signed by Giovanni Battista Rossi.

1691 – Antonio, 13, wrote his early liturgical work *Laetatus sum* (RV Anh 31).
His health was not good - one of his symptoms, *strettezza di petto* ("tightness of the chest"), has been interpreted as a form of asthma.

1693 – Antonio, 15, began studying to become a priest.

1694 – 16 January – Antonio was 15.8 when the 108th Doge Francesco Morosini died (26 February 1619 – 16 January 1694, aged 74.9).
25 February - Silvestro Valiero (Venice, 28 March 1630 – Venice, 7 July 1700, aged 70.3) was the 109th Doge of Venice,

reigning from his election on 25 February 1694 (age 63.9) until his death 6.4 years later.

1 May – Bach was 9 when his mother died.

Il Campanile and Libreria Sansoviniana (left), Palazzo Ducale (center), Palazzo delle Prigioni (center-right).

1695 – 2 March – Bach was 9.9 years old when his father died, 10 months and 1 day after his mother. After becoming an orphan, Bach lived for five years, until 1700, with his eldest brother, Johann Christoph Bach, 24, (1671 – 1721, aged 50), the organist at St. Michael's Church in Ohrdruf (30 km southeast of Eisenach), Saxe-Gotha-Altenburg. There he studied, performed, and copied music, including his own brother's, despite being forbidden to do so, because scores were so valuable and private, and blank ledger paper of that type was costly. He received good teaching from his brother, who instructed him on the clavichord. J.C. Bach shown him the works of great composers of the day, including South German composers such as Johann Pachelbel (1653, Nurenberg, Germany – 3 March 1706, Nurenberg, aged 53, under whom Johann Christoph had studied), and Johann Jakob Froberger (19 May 1616 – 7 May

1667, aged 50.9, 12 days before 51); North German composers; Frenchmen, such as Jean-Baptiste Lully (28 Nov 1632, Florence, Italy - 22 March 1687, aged 54.3, Italian-born French (French subject in 1661, age 29) composer, instrumentalist, and dancer, who worked in the court of King Louis XIV (5 Sep 1638 – 1 Sep 1715, aged 76.9, 4 days before 77, King for 72.3 years: 14 May 1643 (age 4.7) – 1 Sep 1715) of France), Louis Marchand (2 Feb 1669 – 17 Feb 1732, aged 63, French Baroque organist, harpsichordist, and composer), and Marin Marais (31 May 1656 – 15 August 1728, aged 72.2, French composer and viol player, who studied composition with Jean-Baptiste Lully, often conducting his operas); and the Italian clavierist Girolamo Frescobaldi (13 Sep 1583, Ferrara, Italy – 1 March 1643, Roma, Italia, aged 59.5, Italian musician, one of the most important composers of keyboard music). Also during this time, he was taught theology, Latin, Greek, French, and Italian at the local gymnasium in Ohrdruf.

21 November – Antonio was 17.6 when Henry Purcell died, aged 36.2 (10 Sep 1659 – 21 Nov 1695, English composer).

Italy, Venezia, Piazza San Marco, with Basilica San Marco (center), Palazzo Ducale (right), Torre dell'Orologgio (left, 1499)

1700 – Vivaldi was 22 when, with the patronage of the Grand Prince Ferdinando de' Medici, 37, (9 Aug 1663 in Palazzo Pitti, Firenze, Toscana – 31 Oct 1713 in the same Palazzo Pitti, aged 50.2), Bartolomeo Cristofori, 45, (4 May 1655 – 27 Jan 1731 (aged 75.7) hired in 1688 (age 33)), invented the piano.

3 April – Bach, 15, and his school friend Georg Erdmann, 17, were enrolled in the prestigious St. Michael's School in Lüneburg (270 km north of Ohrdruf, some two weeks' travel, probably undertaken mostly on foot). His two years there were critical in teaching Bach a wider range of European culture. In addition to singing in the choir, he played the School's three-manual organ and harpsichords. Bach had access to St. John's Church and possibly used the church's famous organ 147 years old, from 1553, since it was played by his organ teacher Georg Böhm, 39, (2 Sep 1661 – 18 May 1733, aged 73.7). Because of his musical talent, Bach learned much from Böhm while a student in Lüneburg, and also took trips to nearby Hamburg (50 km northwest), where he observed the great North German organist Johann Adam Reincken, 57, (8 Dec 1643 – 24 Nov 1722, aged 78.9, Dutch-German organist and composer. He was one of the most important German composers of the 17th century, a friend of Dieterich Buxtehude (1637 – 9 May 1707, aged 70, Danish-German organist and composer of the Baroque period), and a major influence on Johann Sebastian Bach; however, very few of his works survive to this day). Stauffer reports the discovery in 2005 of the organ tablatures that Bach wrote out of works by Reincken and Dieterich Buxtehude, showing "a disciplined, methodical, well-trained teenager deeply committed to learning his craft".

7 July - the 109th Doge of Venice, Silvestro Valiero died aged 70.3.

17 July - Alvise II Mocenigo (Luigi Mocenigo), 72.5, (Venice, 3 January 1628 – Venice, 6 May 1709, aged 81.3) was elected the 110th doge of Venice; he was doge from this day for 8.8 years, until his death.

1702 – Vivaldi, 24, started working at the Ospedale della Pietà.

Italy, Venezia - The large yacht Vivaldi (left) tied up at the beautiful waterfront Riva dei Sette Martiri, near a bridge over a canal by the Fondamenta Rio della Tana, and Via Giuseppe Garibaldi is in the middle.

1703 – Antonio Vivaldi, 25, was ordained as a Priest in the Roman Catholic Church. He was nicknamed "il Prete Rosso" ("The Red Priest") because of his red hair, a family trait.

January - shortly after graduating from St. Michael's, and after being turned down for the post of organist at Sangerhausen (80 km northeast of Ohrdruf), Bach, 17.7, was appointed court musician in the chapel of Duke Johann Ernst III, 38.5, (22 June 1664 – 10 May 1707, aged 42.9) in Weimar (50 km northeast of Ohrdruf). During his seven-month tenure at Weimar, his reputation as a keyboardist spread so much that he was invited to inspect the new organ, and give the inaugural recital, at the New Church (now Bach Church) in Arnstadt (20 km southwest of Weimar, and 15 km west of Ohrdruf).

August – Bach, 18.4, became the organist at the New Church, with light duties, a relatively generous salary, and a fine new organ. After some time, tension built up between Bach and the authorities. Bach was dissatisfied with the standard of singers in the choir, but he was asked to be more moderate regarding the musical qualities he expected from his students.

September – Vivaldi, 25.4, became Maestro di Violino at the Pio Ospedale della Pietà orphanage in Venice, for 29 years. He was an exceptional violinist. The school was for the education of girls (there were four similar orphanages in Venezia; they were financed by the Republic of Venezia. The boys learned a trade, and had to leave when they reached the age of 15. The girls received a musical education, and the most talented among them stayed and became members of the Ospedale's renowned orchestra and choir (about 40 girls). This Ospedale was in fact a home for the female offspring of noblemen and their numerous romances with their mistresses. The Ospedale was thus well endowed by the anonymous fathers; its furnishings were closed to the luxurious, the young ladies were well looked-after, and the musical standards among the highest in Venice.). Vivaldi composed over 60 sacred vocal music works, and some of his most famous works for the school orchestra, including "Le Quattro stagioni" ("The Four Seasons").

From this year Bach was back in Thuringia, working as a musician for Protestant churches in Arnstadt and Mühlhausen.

Italy, Venezia - The left door on the west façade of Basilica Cattedrale Patriarcale di San Marco. Above the door we can see the Winged Lion, the symbol of St. Mark and of Venice, which holds the book quoting *"Pax Tibi Marce Evangelista Meus"* (Peace to you, Mark, my evangelist).

1704 – Vivaldi, 26, was given a dispensation from celebrating Mass, because of his ill health. Vivaldi said Mass as a priest only a few times, and appeared to have withdrawn from liturgical duties, though he formally remained a member of the priesthood.

The position of teacher of viola all'inglese was added to his duties as violin instructor. The position of *maestro di coro*, which was at one time filled by Vivaldi, required a lot of time and work.

1705 – Vivaldi, 27, has the first collection (Connor Cassara) of his compositions published by Giuseppe Sala: his Opus 1 is a collection of 12 sonatas for two violins and basso continuo, in a conventional style.

Bach, 20, upset his employer by a prolonged absence from Arnstadt: for around four months in 1705–1706 he visited the organist and composer Dieterich Buxtehude, 68, (1637 – 9 May 1707, aged 70, Danish-German organist and composer of the Baroque period), in the northern city of Lübeck (350 km north of Arnstadt, going mostly on foot, therefore about 3 weeks each way)

Italy, Venezia - Libreria Sansoviniana (left), Basilica di San Marco (left back), Palazzo Ducale (center-left), Palazzo delle Prigioni (center-right).

1706 – 3 March - Vivaldi was one day before 28 when the German composer Johann Pachelbel died in Nurenberg, Germany, aged 53 (1653, Nurenberg, Germany – 3 March 1706).

Bach, 21, applied for a post as organist at the Blasius Church (also known as St. Blasius or as *Divi Blasii*) in Mühlhausen (then German, in 1798 Mulhouse becomes part of France, in 1871 again German, in 1919 Mulhouse becomes part of France again, 430 km southwest of Arnstadt, 19 km southwest of the Rhine River (border between France and Germany), 34 km northwest of Basel, Switzerland).

1707 – 25 February - Vivaldi was almost 29 when Carlo Goldoni was born in Venezia (25 Feb 1707, Venezia, - 6 Feb 1793, Paris, aged 85.9, 19 days before 86, a famous playwright).

24 April (Easter) – Bach, 22, is in Mühlhausen. As part of his application, he had a cantata performed on Easter, likely an early version of his *Christ lag in Todes Banden*.

May - Bach's application was accepted.

July – Bach took up the post in Mühlhausen. The position included a significantly higher remuneration, improved conditions, and a better choir.

August – Bach received an inheritance of 50 gulden (more than half his annual salary) from his maternal uncle, Tobias Lämmerhirt.

17 October – Bach, 22.5 married Maria Barbara Bach, 22.9, 5 months older than him, (30 Oct 1684 – 7 July 1720, aged 35.7), his second cousin, at the church from Dornheim, 3 km east of Arnstadt, her hometown and his previous post.

Bach was able to convince the church and town government at Mühlhausen to fund an expensive renovation of the organ at the Blasius Church.

<u>1708</u> – Bach, 23, wrote *Gott ist mein König*, a festive cantata for the inauguration of the new Council in Mühlhausen, which was published at the Council's expense.

Bach left Mühlhausen, and returned to Weimar, this time as organist at the ducal court. Bach and his wife Maria moved into a house close to the ducal palace. Later the same year, their first child, Catharina Dorothea, was born, and Maria Barbara's elder, unmarried sister joined them. She remained to help run the household for 21 years, until her death in 1729, 9 years after the death of her younger sister Maria.

28 December – Bach, 23.7, and his wife Maria, 24.2, had their first child in Weimar, Catharina Dorothea Bach (28 Dec 1708 – 14 Jan 1774, aged 65.1).

Germany - 23 March 1978, Freibourg im Breisgau (1120 by Duke Berthold III of Zähringen (1085-1122), elevation 278 m, the south façade of Freiburger Münster (cathedral, 1200, 116 m, J. S. Bach (1685-1750) performed here).

1709 – Vivaldi, 31, having difficult relationship with some from the board of directors of the Ospedale, had to leave the Ospedale, and became a freelance musician.

A second collection of 12 sonatas for violin and basso continuo appeared — Opus 2.

8 February - Giuseppe Torelli died in Bologna at 50.8 (22 April 1658, Verona – 8 Feb 1709, Italian violist, violinist, teacher, and composer of instrumental concerti, especially concerti grossi, and solo concerti, for strings and continuo, and the most prolific Baroque composer for trumpets).

6 May - the 110th Doge of Venice, Alvise II Mocenigo (Luigi Mocenigo), died, aged 81.3.

22 May - Giovanni II Cornaro, 61.8, (4 August 1647 – 12 August 1722, aged 75 years and 8 days), a Venetian nobleman and statesman, was elected and served as the 111th Doge of Venice from this day for 13.2 years, until his death.

Italy, Venezia - On the west façade of Palazzo Ducale, above the Porta della Carta, we see the Winged Lion and on top raises a statue of Justice.

1710 – 4 January - Giovanni Battista Pergolesi was born (4 Jan 1710 – 16 March 1736, aged 26.2, Italian composer, violinist and organist; his best-known works include his Stabat Mater and the opera *La serva padrona* (*The Maid Turned Mistress*)).

22 November – Bach, 25.6, and his wife Maria, 26.1, had their second child in Weimar, Wilhelm Friedemann Bach (22 Nov 1710 – 1 July 1784, aged 73.6).

1711 – Vivaldi, 33, was recalled by the board of directors of the Ospedale, with a unanimous vote.

February - Vivaldi and his father traveled to Brescia, where his setting of the Stabat Mater (RV 621) was played as part of a religious festival.

He published his first collection of 12 concerti for one, two, and four violins with strings, *L'estro armonico* (Opus 3, Harmonic Inspiration), which was published in Amsterdam by Estienne Roger, 46, (1665 – 7 July 1722, aged 57, francophone printer and publisher working in Amsterdam, whose distribution was well-organized. He had, for example, a distributor in Leipzig, with whom Bach was in regular contact. Bach indeed adapted a number of Vivaldi's works for organ and harpsichord, and as concertos for harpsichord and strings. He also included several of Vivaldi's works during the popular musical evenings, which he organized during the 1730s at Zimmerman's Coffee House in Leipzig), dedicated to Grand Prince Ferdinando de' Medici, 48, (9 Aug 1663 in Palazzo Pitti, Firenze, Toscana – 31 Oct 1713 in the same Palazzo Pitti, aged 50.2, Prince for 43.4 years: 23 May 1670 (age 6.7) – 31 Oct 1713; with his patronage, Bartolomeo Cristofori was hired in 1688, and invented the piano around 1700) of Toscana. The prince sponsored many musicians including Alessandro Scarlatti (2 May 1660 – 22 Oct 1725, aged 65.4), his son Domenico Scarlatti (26 Oct 1685 – 23 July 1757, aged 71.7) and George Frideric Handel (5 March 1685 – 14 April 1759, aged 74.1, burial place Westminster Abbey, London). He was a musician himself, and Vivaldi probably met him in Venice. *L'estro armonico* was a resounding success all over Europe.

12 October – Holy Roman (Austrian) Emperor Charles VI, 26, started his reign.

22 December – Coronation of Holy Roman (Austrian) Emperor Charles VI in Frankfurt.

Italy, Venezia - Two of the four horses on the Basilica di San Marco, brought by Doge Enrico Dandolo in 1204, and installed around 1254.

1712 – 28 June – Vivaldi was 34.2 when Jean-Jacques Rousseau was born in Geneva, Switzerland (28 June 1712, – 2 July 1778, Ermenonville, France, aged 65.9, 4 days before 66, Genevan philosopher, writer, and composer).

Bach's (27) time in Weimar was the start of a sustained period of composing keyboard and orchestral works. He included influences from abroad, like dramatic openings, dynamic rhythms, and harmonic schemes found in the music of Italians, such as Vivaldi, Corelli, and Giuseppe Torelli (22 April 1658, Verona – 8 Feb 1709, Bologna, aged 50.8). Bach learned these stylistic aspects in part by transcribing Vivaldi's string and wind concertos, for harpsichord and organ; many of these transcribed works are still regularly performed. Bach was particularly attracted to the Italian style in which one or more solo instruments alternate section-by-section with the full orchestra throughout a movement.

1713 – 8 January – Vivaldi was 34.8 when Arcangelo Corelli died at 59.9 (17 February 1653 – 8 January 1713, Italian violinist and composer of the Baroque era, older contemporaneous with Giuseppe Torelli (Corelli was born 5.2 years before Torelli, and died 3.9 years after him)).

Vivaldi started his career as an opera composer as a sideline: his first opera, *Ottone in villa* (RV 729) was performed at the Garzerie Theater in Vicenza (50 km west of Venezia).

23 February – Bach, 27.9, and his wife Maria, 28.3, had their third child in Weimar, Johann Christoph Bach (23 Feb 1713 – 23 Feb 1713, died after birth).

23 February – Bach, 27.9, and his wife Maria, 28.3, had their fourth child in Weimar, Maria Sophia Bach (23 Feb 1713 – 15 March 1713, died after 20 days, twin of Johann Christoph Bach).

Bach started work on the *Little Organ Book*, containing traditional Lutheran chorale tunes set in complex textures.

Bach was offered a post in Halle (founded in 806, 70 km northeast of Weimar), when he advised the authorities during a renovation by Christoph Cuntzius of the main organ in the west gallery of the Market Church of Our Dear Lady.

1714 – Vivaldi, 36, published *La stravaganza* (Opus 4), a collection of concerti for solo violin and strings, dedicated to an old violin student of Vivaldi's, the Venetian noble Vettor Dolfin.

Vivaldi became the impresario of the Teatro Sant' Angelo in Venice, where his opera *Orlando finto pazzo* (RV 727) was performed for a couple of weeks. He also produced an opera by the young composer Giovanni Alberto Rostori, 22, (1692-1753, aged 61).

8 March – Bach, 28.9 and his wife Maria, 29.2, had their fifth child, in Weimar, Carl Philipp Emanuel Bach (8 March 1714 – 14 Dec 1788, aged 74.7, great composer himself). Georg Philipp Telemann, almost 33, was the godfather and namesake of Bach's son.

Bach, 29, was promoted to *Konzertmeister* (director of music) at the ducal court in Weimar, where he had an opportunity to work with a large, well-funded group of professional musicians. He performed a church cantata monthly in the castle church. The first three cantatas in the new series Bach composed in Weimar were

Himmelskönig, sei willkommen, BWV 182, for Palm Sunday, which coincided with the Annunciation that year, *Weinen, Klagen, Sorgen, Zagen*, BWV 12, for Jubilate Sunday, and *Erschallet, ihr Lieder, erklinget, ihr Saiten!* BWV 172 for Pentecost. Bach's first Christmas cantata *Christen, ätzet diesen Tag*, BWV 63 was premiered in 1714.

Bach attended the service at the St. Thomas church in Leipzig, on the first Sunday of Advent.

1715 – Vivaldi, 37, presented *Nerone fatto Cesare* (RV 724, now lost), with music by seven different composers, of which he was the leader. The opera contained eleven arias, and was a success. In the late season, Vivaldi planned to put on an opera entirely of his own creation, *Arsilda, Regina di Ponto* (RV 700), but the state censor blocked the performance.

11 May – Bach, 30.1 and his wife Maria, 30.5, had their sixth child in Weimar, Johann Gottfried Bernhard Bach (11 May 1715 – 27 May 1739, aged 24).

Italy, Venezia - Palazzo Dandolo on Riva degli Schiavoni, 150 m east of Piazza San Marco.

1716 – Vivaldi, 38, became responsible for all of the musical activity of the Ospedale, when he was promoted to *maestro de' concerti* (music director).

Vivaldi got the censor to accept the opera *Arsilda, Regina di Ponto*, and it was a resounding success.

The Ospedale della Pietà commissioned several liturgical works for Vivaldi. The most important were two oratorios. *Moyses Deus Pharaonis*, (RV 643) is now lost. The second, *Juditha triumphans devicta Holofernis barbaric* (RV 644), celebrates the victory of the Republic of Venice against the Turks and the recapture of the island of Corfu (20 August 1716). Composed immediately after the victory, and performed in November, it is one of his sacred masterpieces. All eleven singing parts were performed by girls of the orphanage, both the female and male roles. Many of the arias include parts for solo instruments — recorders, oboes, violas d'amore, and mandolins — that showcased the range of talents of the girls. Also Vivaldi wrote and produced two more operas, *L'incoronazione di Dario* (RV 719) and *La costanza trionfante degli amori e degli odi* (RV 706). The latter was so popular that it performed two years later, re-edited and retitled *Artabano re dei Parti* (RV 701, now lost). In the years that followed, Vivaldi wrote several operas that were performed all over Italy.

Bach, 31, and Johann Kuhnau (Thomaskantor in Leipzig from 1701 until his death on 5 June 1722) had met on the occasion of the testing and inauguration of an organ in Halle.

1717 – 6 November - Bach, 32.6, had some disagreements in Weimar, and was jailed for 26 days.

2 December – Bach was freed from arrest, with notice of his unfavorable discharge.

Leopold, Prince of Anhalt-Köthen, 23, (28 Nov 1694 – 19 Nov 1728, aged 33.9, 9 days before 34), hired Bach to serve as his *Kapellmeister* (director of music) in Köthen (30 km north of Halle). Prince Leopold, himself a musician, appreciated Bach's talents, paid him well, and gave him considerable latitude in composing and performing. The prince was Calvinist and did not use elaborate music in his worship; accordingly, most of Bach's work from this period was secular, including the orchestral suites, the cello suites, the sonatas and partitas for solo violin, and the *Brandenburg Concertos*. Bach also composed secular cantatas for the court such as *Die Zeit, die Tag und Jahre macht*, BWV 134a. A significant influence upon Bach's musical development, during his years with the Prince, was the dance music, which was second only to his adoption of Vivaldi's music in Weimar.

Bach tested the organ of the *Paulinerkirche* in Leipzig.

Germany, Freibourg im Breisgau, 510 km southwest from Brunswick, 23 March 1978, the Historical Merchants' Hall of 1520-1530, façade decorated with statues and the coat of arms of four Habsburg (1027-1780) emperors, in Freibourg im Breisgau (1120 by Duke Berthold III of Zähringen (1085-1122), elevation 278 m, population 222,000, area 153 km^2), southwest Germany, near France and Switzerland.

1718 – Vivaldi, 40, had frequent travels from this year on, but the Ospedale paid him 2 sequins (or ducats, about $300 now) to write two concerti a month for the orchestra, and to rehearse with them at least five times when in Venice.

Vivaldi was offered a prestigious new position as *Maestro di Cappella* (Chamber Capellmeister) at the court of prince Landgrave Philip van Hessen-Darmstadt, 47, (20 July 1671 in Darmstadt (575 km northwest of Venezia) – 11 August 1736 in Vienna (435 km northeast of Venezia), aged 65 and 22 days) Prince of Hesse-Darmstadt, Imperial Field marshal, and Governor of Mantua (125 km southwest of Venezia). He moved to Mantua for three years (1718 – 1720).

15 November – Bach, 33.6 and his wife Maria, 34, had their seventh child in Köthen, Leopold Augustus Bach (15 Nov 1718 – 29 Sep 1719, died after 10 months and 14 days).

1719 – Vivaldi, 41, in Matua, produced several operas, among them Armida, Teuzzone, and Tito Manlio (RV 738; on the score of this opera are the words: "music by Vivaldi, made in 5 days.").

Vivaldi became acquainted with an aspiring young singer Anna Tessieri Girò (or Giraud) (circa 1710 in Mantua – 1750, aged 40, Italian mezzo-soprano, debuted in 1723 (age 13), and she was a prima donna for 22 years, until 1748 (age 38), when she married a Count, and retired from performing), who would become his student this year (age 10), protégée (age 14), and favorite *prima donna* (age 16). Anna, 32 years younger than Vivaldi, along with her older half-sister Paolina, moved in to live with him, became part of Vivaldi's entourage, and regularly accompanied him on his many travels. There was speculation as to the nature of Vivaldi's and Girò's relationship, but no evidence exists to indicate anything beyond friendship, and professional collaboration. Vivaldi maintained that she was no more than a housekeeper and good friend, just like Anna's half-sister, Paolina, who also shared his house. In his Memoirs, written around 1790, the Italian playwright Carlo Goldoni (25 Feb 1707, Venezia, - 6 Feb 1793, Paris, aged 85.9, 19 days before 86; he worked with Vivaldi, 29 years older than him, after 1729) gave the following portrait of Vivaldi and Giraud, probably from 1729 (Vivaldi 51, Giraud 19, Goldoni 22): "This priest, an excellent violinist, has trained Miss Giraud to be a singer. She was young, born in Venice (in reality Mantua), but the daughter of a French wigmaker. She was not beautiful, though she was elegant, small in stature, with beautiful eyes, and a fascinating mouth. She had a small voice, but many languages in which to harangue." Vivaldi stayed together with her most of the time.

George Frideric Handel was born 26 days before Bach, in Halle-upon-Saale (130 km northeast of Eisenach, and 30 km south of Köthen) (5 March 1685 – 14 April 1759, aged 74.1, burial place Westminster Abbey, London). Despite being of the same age, and living less than 130 km apart, Bach and Handel never met. In 1719, Bach made the 30-km south journey from Köthen to Halle, with the intention of meeting Handel, however, Handel had left the town.

London - From The Mall, looking southwest to the Victoria Memorial (1911, center left) and to the Buckingham Palace (1703).

1720 – Vivaldi, 42, in Mantua, performed "La Conduce o siano Li veri amici".

Vivaldi returned to Venice, where he again staged new operas written by himself in the Teatro Sant' Angelo.

7 July – While Bach, 35.3, was away in Karlsbad (400 km southwest of Köthen) with Prince Leopold, 26, his wife Maria suddenly died at 35.7. He remained with four children: Catharina 11.5, Wilhelm 9.6, Carl 6.3, and Johann 5.1.

1721 – Vivaldi, 43, was in Milano (250 km west of Venezia), where he presented the pastoral drama *La Silvia* (RV 734); nine arias from it survive.

3 December – Bach, 36.7, married Anna Magdalena Wilcke, 20.2, (22 Sep 1701 – 22 Feb 1760, aged 58 years and 5 months, soprano who performed at the court in Köthen). They had 13 children.

Italy, Venezia - In the middle of the west façade of the Basilica di San Marco, we see the central bronze-fashioned door, in a round-arched portal, encircled by polychrome marble columns. Above this door there are three round bas-relief cycles of Romanesque art. A Japanese couple, with their Japanese photographer, make their wedding photographs in this most beautiful place.

1722 – 12 August - Vivaldi was 44.4 when the 111th Doge of Venice, Giovanni II Cornaro, died, aged 75 years and 8 days.

24 August - Alvise III Sebastiano Mocenigo, 5 days before 60, (29 August 1662 – 21 May 1732, aged 69.7) was elected the 112th Doge of Venice; he served for 9.7 years, until his death. He was also *Provveditore Generale* (Governor) of Venetian Dalmatia twice.

Vivaldi visited Milano again with the oratorio *L'adorazione delli tre re magi al bambino Gesù* (RV 645, now lost).

Then he moved to Rome, where he introduced his operas' new style.

Bach, 37, who began to write the preludes and fugues 12 years ago, had them assembled into the first book of his monumental work *The Well-Tempered Clavier* (*Das Wohltemperierte Klavier*—"*Klavier*" meaning clavichord or harpsichord), containing 24 preludes and fugues in every major and minor key. The second book will be published in 1744.

Italy, Venezia - The Piazzetta dei Leoncini, on the north side of the Basilica, with two marble lions (offered by Doge Alvise Mocenigo in 1722).

1723 – Vivaldi, 45, composed "Le Quattro Stagioni" ("The Four Seasons") - four violin concertos that give musical expression to the seasons of the year. Though three of the concerti are wholly original, the first, "Primavera (Spring)", borrows motifs from a Sinfonia in the first act of Vivaldi's contemporaneous opera *Il Giustino*. The inspiration for the concertos was probably the countryside around Mantua, where he was 4 years ago. They were a big novelty in musical conception: in them Vivaldi represented flowing creeks, singing birds (of different species, each specifically characterized), barking dogs, buzzing mosquitoes, crying shepherds, storms, drunken dancers, silent nights, hunting parties from both the hunters' and the prey's point of view, frozen landscapes, ice-skating children, and warming winter fires. Each concerto is associated with a sonnet, possibly by Vivaldi, describing the scenes depicted in the music.

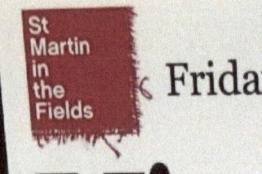

London - The program by Candlelight at St Martin in the Fields, on Friday, Oct. 14, 2016 at 7:30 PM, with Antonio Vivaldi (1678 in Venice-1741 (age 63) Vienna), Johann Sebastian Bach (1685-1750 (age 65)), Francesco Geminiani (1687-1762 (age 75)), George Frideric Handel (1685 Germany-1759 (age 74) London), Wolfgang Amadeus Mozart (1756 Salzburg-1791 (age 35) Vienna), Johann Pachelbel (1653 Nuremberg-1706 (age 53) Nuremberg, Germany).

The orphanage's records show that he was paid for 140 concerti (about $21,000 now) between 1723 and 1733.

Bach, 38, was appointed *Thomaskantor*, Cantor of the *Thomasschule* at the *Thomaskirche* (St. Thomas Church) in Leipzig (founded 1015, 50 km southeast of Köthen, and 80 km northeast of Weimar), which provided music for four churches in the city, the *Thomaskirche*, the *Nikolaikirche* (St. Nicholas Church), and to a lesser extent the *Neue Kirche* (New Church), and the *Peterskirche* (St. Peter's Church). This was "the leading cantorate in Protestant Germany", located in the mercantile city in the Electorate of Saxony, which he held for twenty-seven years until his death. During that time he gained further prestige through honorary appointments at the courts of Köthen and Weissenfels, as well as that of the Elector Frederick Augustus (who was also King of Poland) in Dresden. Bach frequently disagreed with his employer, Leipzig's city council. He composed music for the principal churches of the city, and for its university's student ensemble Collegium Musicum.

After having been offered the position, Bach was invited to Leipzig only after Georg Philipp Telemann, 42, (24 March 1681 – 25 June 1767, German Baroque composer and multi-instrumentalist) indicated that he would not be interested in relocating to Leipzig. Telemann went to (Hamburg 300 km northwest from Leipzig) where he had his own struggles with the city's senate.

30 May - The first cantata performed was *Die Elenden sollen essen*, BWV 75, in the *Nikolaikirche*, the first Sunday after Trinity. Bach usually led performances of his cantatas, most of which were composed within three years of his relocation to Leipzig. Bach collected his cantatas in annual cycles. Five are mentioned in obituaries, three are surviving. Of the more than three hundred cantatas which Bach composed in Leipzig, over one hundred have been lost to posterity.

Bach, 38, and his wife Anna, 22, had their first child, in Leipzig, and Bach's eight child, Christina Sophia Henrietta Bach (1723 – 1726, aged 3).

Italy, Venezia - The Clock Tower (Torre dell'Orologio), 1499. At the top there are two bronze figures, which strike the hours on a bell. The bell was casted at the Arsenal in 1497. Below is the winged lion of Venice. There was a statue of the Doge Agostino Barbarigo (Doge 1486-1501) before the lion. Below the statues of the Virgin and Child. On either side are two large blue panels showing the time: 5:55 PM, the same on the clock below: XVII very close to XVIII.

1724 – Spring – Vivaldi, 46, was active in Rome, where he found a patron in the person of Cardinal Pietro Ottoboni, 57, (2 July 1667, Venezia – 29 Feb 1740, Roma, aged 72.7, grandnephew of Pope Alexander VIII (22 April 1610 – 1 Feb 1691, aged 80.8, born Pietro Vito Ottoboni)), a great patron of music and art, who earlier had been the patron of Arcangelo Corelli (17 February 1653 – 8 January 1713, Italian violinist and composer of the Baroque era).

Summer – Vivaldi was 46.2 when the new Pope Benedict XIII, 75.3, (2 Feb 1649 – 21 Feb 1730, aged 81 and 19 days), Pope for 5.7 years (29 May 1724 – 21 Feb 1730), invited him to play at Pope's residence.

Over 60 years before, around 1663, musical life in Rome had been stimulated by the presence in the city of Christina of Sweden (18 Dec 1626, Tre Kronor – 19 April 1689, Roma, aged 62.3, Queen of Sweden for 21 years and 7 months, from 6 Nov 1632 (age 5.9, coronation 20 Oct 1650, age 23.8) until her abdication on 6 June 1654 (age 27.5), daughter of King Gustavus II Adolphus of Sweden (9 Dec 1594, Stockholm – 6 Nov 1632, Lutzen, Germany, aged 37.9, King for 21 years from 1611 (age 16.9) to 1632, founder of Sweden as a great power). The "Pallas of the North" was her nickname. Around 1663 she (age 37) moved to Rome, and took up residence in the Palazzo Riario. There she organized musical events that were attended by composers younger than her, such as Arcangelo Corelli (17 February 1653 – 8 January 1713, Italian violinist and composer of the Baroque era), and Alessandro Scarlatti (2 May 1660 – 22 Oct 1725, aged 65.4).

Bach started a second annual cycle the first Sunday after Trinity of 1724 and composed only chorale cantatas, each based on a single church hymn. These include *O Ewigkeit, du Donnerwort*, BWV 20, *Wachet auf, ruft uns die Stimme*, BWV 140, *Nun komm, der Heiden Heiland*, BWV 62, and *Wie schön leuchtet der Morgenstern*, BWV 1.

Bach, 39, and his wife Anna, 23, had their second child, and Bach's ninth child, Gottfried Heinrich Bach (1724 – 1763, aged 39).

Italy, Roma - Trajan's column was erected in 113 AD in honor of Emperor Trajan. It is located at the Forum of Trajan. The column commemorates Trajan's victories in Dacia (now Romania), and is 42 meters tall, including its base.

1725 – Vivaldi, 47, returned to Venice, where he produced four operas in the same year.

"Le Quattro Stagioni" ("The Four Seasons") were published as the first four concertos in a collection of twelve (including Storm at Sea, Pleasure and The Hunt.), *Il cimento dell'armonia e dell'inventione*, Opus 8, in Amsterdam, by Michel-Charles Le Cène, 41, (1684 – 1743, aged 59, French printer). These concertos were enormously successful, particularly in France.

22 October - Vivaldi was 47.6 when Alessandro Scarlatti died, aged 65.4 (2 May 1660 – 22 Oct 1725).

The *serenata* (cantata) *Gloria e Imeneo* (RV 687) was commissioned by the French ambassador to Venice, in celebration of the marriage of Louis XV, 15, (15 Feb 1710, Palais de Versailles, France – 10 May 1774, same place, aged 64.2, Reign 1 Sep 1715 (5.5 years) – 10 May 1774) with Marie Leszczyńska, 22, (23 June 1703 – 24 June 1768, aged 65 and 1 day). "Primavera (Spring)" from Le Quattro Stagioni was also a great favorite of King Louis XV, who would order it to be performed at the most unexpected moments, and Vivaldi received various commissions for further compositions from the court at Versailles.

Bach, 40, and his wife Anna, 24, had their third child, and Bach's tenth child, Christian Gottlieb Bach (1725 – 1728, aged 3).

1726 – Vivaldi, 48, despite his stay in Rome and other cities, he remained in the service of the Ospedale della Pietà, which nominated him "Maestro di concerti." He was required only to send two concertos per month to Venice (transport costs were to the account of the client), for which he received a ducat per concerto. His presence was not required. He also remained director of the Teatro Sant' Angelo, as he did in this year, next year 1727, and 1728 seasons. Between 1725 and 1728 some eight operas were premiered in Venice and Florence. Antonio Schinella Conti (22 Jan 1677, Padua – 6 April 1749, Padua, aged 72.2), also known by his religious title as Abate Conti, was an Italian mathematician, writer, translator, philosopher and physicist. In 1699 Conti, 22, became an Oratorian Father in Venice. He wrote of his younger (by just a little more than one year) contemporary, Vivaldi: "In less than three months Vivaldi has composed three operas, two for Venice and a third for Florence;

the last has given something of a boost to the name of the theater of that city, and he has earned a great deal of money."

From this year Bach, 41, published some of his keyboard and organ music.

Bach, 41, and his wife Anna, 25, had their fourth child, and Bach's 11th child, Elisabeth Juliana Friederica Bach (1726 – 1781, aged 55, called Liesgen, married to Bach's pupil Johann Christoph Altnickol in January 1749).

1727 – Vivaldi, 49, composed the "Stabat Mater", based on the hymn "The Sorrows of Mary", for solo alto voice and strings. It is a masterpiece of simplicity.

31 March – Sir Isaac Newton died in London, aged 84.2. Resting Place – Westminster Abbey.

The upper part of the western façade and entrance of Westminster Abbey (960, 1517, Anglican abbey with daily services, and all coronations since 1066, tower height 69 m).

August - Vivaldi wrote another *serenata*, *La Sena festeggiante* (RV 694, Festival on the Seine), for and premiered at the French embassy as well, celebrating the birth of the French royal twin princesses, Louise Élisabeth (14 August 1727 – 6 Dec 1759, aged 32.3) and Henriette (14 August 1727 – 10 Feb 1752, aged 24.5).

Bach, 42, and his wife Anna, 26, had their 5th child, and Bach's 12th child, Ernestus Andreas Bach (1727 – 1727, died shortly after birth).

1728 – While visiting Trieste (120 km northeast of Venezia), Vivaldi, 50, was knighted by the Holy Roman (Austrian) Emperor Charles VI, 43, (1 Oct 1685 – 20 Oct 1740 (aged 55 and 19 days), Reign 12 Oct 1711 – 20 Oct 1740 (29 years)), and invited to visit Vienna. Vivaldi met the Emperor while the Emperor was visiting Trieste to oversee the construction of a new port. Emperor Charles VI admired the music of Vivaldi so much that he is said to have spoken more with the composer during their one meeting, than he spoke to his ministers in over two years. He gave Vivaldi the title of knight, a gold medal, and an invitation to Vienna. Vivaldi gave Emperor Charles VI a manuscript copy of *La cetra*, a set of concerti almost completely different from the set of the same title published as Opus 9. Probably because the printing was not ready, Vivaldi had to gather an improvised collection for the Emperor.

Bach, 43, and his wife Anna, 27, had their 6th child, and Bach's 13th child, Regina Johanna Bach (1728 – 1733, aged 5).

1729 – La Griselda is an opera composed by Vivaldi, 51, based on a libretto written by Carlo Goldoni, 22, (25 Feb 1707, Venezia, - 6 Feb 1793, Paris, aged 85.9, 19 days before 86), a famous playwright, from an earlier libretto by Apostolo Zeno.

March – Bach, 44, broadened his composing and performing beyond the liturgy by taking over the directorship of the Collegium Musicum, a secular performance ensemble started by Telemann, 48. Year round, Leipzig's *Collegium Musicum* performed regularly in venues such as the Café Zimmermann, a coffeehouse on Catherine Street, off the main market square. Many of Bach's works during the 1730s and 1740s were written for and performed by the *Collegium Musicum*; among these were parts of his *Clavier-Übung* (*Keyboard Practice*), and many of his violin and keyboard concertos.

Bach, 44, and his wife Anna, 28, had their 7th child, and Bach's 14th child, Christina Benedicta Bach (1729 – 1730, aged 1).

First wife Maria Barbara's elder, unmarried sister, who remained to help run the Bach's household for 21 years, from 1708, died.

1730 – Vivaldi, 52, accompanied by his father (around 75 years old), and Anna Giraud (20) traveled to Vienna and Prague (550 km northeast of Venezia), where his opera *Farnace* (RV 711) was presented in the spring. In Prague (half a century later Mozart would celebrate his first operatic triumphs there), Vivaldi met a Venetian opera company, which between 1724 and 1734 staged some sixty operas in the theater of Count Franz Anton von Sporck (for whom incidentally, Bach produced his Four Shorter Masses). In the Sep 1730 – May 1731 season, two new operas by Vivaldi were premiered there, after the previous season had closed with his opera Farnace, a work the composer often used as his showpiece.

Some of his later operas were created in collaboration with two of Italy's major writers of the time. *L'Olimpiade* and *Catone in Utica* were written by Pietro Metastasio, 32, (3 Jan 1698 – 12 April 1782, aged 84.2), the major representative of the Arcadian movement and court poet in Vienna.

Bach's, 45, oldest son Wilhelm Friedemann, 20, travelled to Halle to invite Handel, 45, to visit the Bach family in Leipzig, but the visit did not come to pass.

1731 – December - Vivaldi, 53.7, returned to Venezia.

Bach, 46, and his wife Anna, 30, had their 8th child, and Bach's 15th child, Christina Dorothea Bach (1731 – 1732, aged 1).

1732 – 24 Jan, in Paris, Pierre-Augustin Caron de Beaumarchais was born. He will be a French polymath. At various times in his life, he will be a watchmaker, inventor, playwright (Le Barbier de Séville, Le Mariage de Figaro), musician, diplomat, spy, publisher, horticulturist, arms dealer (from France to Washington), satirist, financier, and revolutionary (both French and American). He will die just 6 months and 26 days before Washington, in 1799, at 67.3.

22 February: George Washington was born in Westmoreland County, Virginia, south of Potomac River (60 km south of Washington, DC).

The king of the British Empire, including the American colonies, was George II (George Augustus, 1683-1760 (aged 76.99 (just 5 days before 77)), king 1727 (43.7 years old) - 25 Oct 1760 (76.99, 33.3 years king), had 8 children), now 48.3.

The King of France was Louis XV the Beloved (1710-1774, aged 64.2, King 1715 (age 5.6) - 21 Sep 1774, for 58.6 years), now 22 years old.

Spring – Vivaldi, 54, left again for Mantua and Verona. In Mantua, Vivaldi's opera Semimmide was performed, and in Verona, on the occasion of the opening of the new Teatro Filarmonico, La fida Ninfa, with a libretto by the Veronese poet and man of letters, Francesco Scipione, marchese di Maffei, or Scipione Maffei (1 June 1675, Verona – 11 Feb 1755, Verona, aged 79.7, Italian writer contemporaneous with Vivaldi (he was born 2.8 years before Vivaldi, and died 13.6 years after him)), was staged.

Italia, Verona - 28 Sept 2008, from Piazza Bra, looking southeast to Arena di Verona (Roman amphitheater built in 30 AD for 30,000 people (now limited to 15,000, with opera performances starting in 1913 (Aida by Giuseppe Verdi), and continuing to this day)), with people dressed as Roman soldiers, in front of Biglietteria (tickets).

31 March – Joseph Haydn was born (31 March 1732 – 31 May 1809, aged 77 years and 2 months, an Austrian composer of the Classical period. He was a friend and mentor of Mozart (27 January 1756 – 5 December 1791, aged 35 years, 10 months and 8 days), a teacher of Beethoven (17 Dec 1770 – 26 March 1827, aged 56 years, 3 months and 9 days), and the older brother of composer Michael Haydn (14 Sep 1737 – 10 August 1806, aged 68.9).

21 May – Vivaldi was 54 when the 112th Doge of Venice, Alvise III Sebastiano Mocenigo, died, aged 69.7.

6 June - Carlo Ruzzini, 78.6, (11 November 1653 – 5 January 1735, aged 81.1), a Venetian diplomat and statesman, was elected the 113th Doge of Venice, and served for 2.5 years, until his death.

Vivaldi's opera *Artabano re dei Parti* (RV 701, now lost) was performed in Prague.

Bach, 47, and his wife Anna, 31, had their 9th child, and Bach's 16th child, Johann Christoph Friedrich Bach (1732 – 1795, aged 63, musician called the Bückeburg Bach).

Paris - On the façade of l'Opéra de Paris (1875): a statue and the bust of Franz Joseph Haydn (1732 – 1809), prolific and important Austrian Composer. He signed his musical work in Italian: "di me giuseppe Haydn" (by me Joseph Haydn). He wrote a great number of concertos, masses, operas, piano trios, solo piano compositions, string quartets, symphonies, baritone trios, and Gott erhalte Franz den Kaiser, which was used in Das Lied der Deutschen – Germany's national anthem.

1733 – Vivaldi, 55, concentrated mainly on operas. No further collections of instrumental music were published. However Vivaldi continued to write instrumental music, although it was only to sell the manuscripts to private persons, or to the Ospedale della Pietà. This year he met the English traveler, Edward Holdsworth, who had been commissioned to purchase a few of Vivaldi's compositions for the man of letters, Charles Jennens, 33, (1700 – 20 Nov 1773, aged 73, English landowner and patron of the arts. As a friend of Handel, he helped author the libretti of several of his oratorios, most notably Messiah). Holdsworth wrote to Jennens: "I spoke with your friend Vivaldi today. He told me that he had decided to publish no more concertos, because otherwise he can no longer sell his handwritten compositions. He earns more with these, he said, and since he charges one guinea ($140) per piece, that must be true if he finds a goodly number of buyers."

Bach, 48, composed a mass for the Dresden (100 km southeast of Leipzig) court (*Kyrie* and *Gloria*), which he later incorporated in his *Mass in Re (B) Minor*. He presented the manuscript to the Elector Frederick Augustus II, 37, (17 Oct 1696, Dresden – 5 Oct 1763, Dresden, aged 66.9, 12 days before 67) in an eventually successful bid to persuade the prince to give him the title of Court Composer. He later extended this work into a full mass, by adding a Credo, Sanctus', and Agnus Dei, the music for which was partly based on his own cantatas, partly newly composed.

Bach, 48, and his wife Anna, 32, had their 10th child, and Bach's 17th child, Johann August Abraham Bach (1733 – 1733, died shortly after birth).

1735 –5 January – Vivaldi was 56.8 when the 113th Doge of Venice, Carlo Ruzzini, died, aged 81.1.

17 January - Alvise Pisani, 71 and 16 days, (1 January 1664 in Venice – 17 June 1741 in Venice, aged 77.5) was elected the 114th Doge of Venice, serving from this day, for 6 years and 5 months, until his death.

After 1735 Ospedale della Pietà paid Vivaldi a fixed honorarium of 100 ducats ($14,000) a year.

Bach started to prepare his first publication of organ music, which was printed as third *Clavier-Übung* in 1739.

Bach, 50, and his wife Anna, 34, had their 11th child, and Bach's 18th child, Johann Christian Bach (1735 – 1782, aged 46.3, significant musician called the London Bach).

1736 – Vivaldi was 58 when Bach, 51, was granted the title of court composer by the Elector of Saxony and King of Poland.

16 March - Giovanni Battista Pergolesi died of tuberculosis at the very young age of 26 years 2 months and 12 days (4 Jan 1710 – 16 March 1736, Italian composer, violinist and organist; his best-known works include his Stabat Mater and the opera *La serva padrona* (*The Maid Turned Mistress*)).

1737 – Vivaldi, 59, in a letter written to his patron Marchese Bentivoglio, makes reference to his "94 operas". Only around 50 operas by Vivaldi have been discovered, and no other documentation of the remaining operas exists – it is possible that he refers to 44 operas which he produced as impresario.

14 September - Michael Haydn was born (14 Sep 1737 – 10 August 1806, aged 68.9).

16 November - Vivaldi, 59.6, unwaveringly denied any romantic relationship with his student and preferred prima donna Anna Girò, 27, in a letter to his patron Bentivoglio.

Antonio Stradivari died at 93 (1644 – 1737).

Bach, 52, and his wife Anna, 36, had their 12th child, and Bach's 19th child, Johanna Carolina Bach (1737 – 1781, aged 44).

Between 1737 and 1739, Bach's former pupil Carl Gotthelf Gerlach held the directorship of the *Collegium Musicum*.

1738 – Vivaldi, 60, was in Amsterdam where he conducted a festive opening concert for the 100th Anniversary of the Schouwburg Theatre.

Netherlands, 14 Aug 1977, Amsterdam (1275, population 1.3 M, elevation minus 2 m (2 m under the Atlantic Ocean level)): Zijkanaal G, with a bridge for the street s150, and Havenstraat on the left.

1739 – Bach, 54, had his first publication of organ music, which was printed as third *Clavier-Übung*.

He started to compile and compose the set of preludes and fugues for harpsichord that would become his second book of *The Well-Tempered Clavier*.

1740 – In the spring, Vivaldi, 62, resigned from the Pio Ospedale della Pietà orphanage in Venice, and moved to Vienna, invited by the Holy Roman (Austrian) Emperor Charles VI, 54.5. On his way to Vienna, Vivaldi may have stopped in Graz (300 km northeast of Venezia), to see his former student Anna Girò, 30. Probably that Vivaldi went to Vienna to stage operas, especially as he took up residence near the Kärntnertortheater.

From this year to 1748 Bach copied, transcribed, expanded and programmed music in an older polyphonic style (*stile antico*), by, among others,

- Giovanni Pierluigi da Palestrina (1525 – 2 Feb 1594, aged 69, Italian Renaissance composer of sacred music, and the best-known 16th-century representative of the Roman School of musical composition. He had a lasting influence on the development of church music, and his work has often been seen as the culmination of Renaissance polyphony) (BNB I/P/2),
- Johann Caspar Kerll (9 April – 13 Feb 1693, aged 65.8, German baroque composer and organist) (BWV 241),
- Pietro Torri (1650 in Peschiera del Garda – 6 July 1737, aged 87, Italian Baroque composer) (BWV Anh. 30),
- Giovanni Battista Bassani (c. 1650 in Padua – 1 Oct 1716, aged 66, Italian composer, violinist, and organist) (BWV 1081),
- Francesco Gasparini (19 March 1661 – 22 March 1727, aged 66, Italian Baroque composer and teacher) (*Missa Canonica*) and
- Antonio Caldara (1670 in Venice – 28 Dec 1736, Vienna, aged 66, Italian Baroque composer) (BWV 1082).

Bach's own style shifted in the last decade of his life, showing an increased integration of polyphonic structures and canons, and other elements of the *stile antico.*

20 October – death of the Holy Roman (Austrian) Emperor Charles VI, (1 Oct 1685 – 20 Oct 1740 (aged 55 and 19 days), Reign 12 Oct 1711 – 20 Oct 1740 (29 years)).

Girolamo Amati died 5 days before 91 (Hieronymus II, 26 Feb 1649 - 21 Feb 1740, the last of the Amati family of luthiers).

1741 – 17 June - the 114th Doge of Venice, Alvise Pisani, died, aged 77.5).

30 June - Pietro Grimani, 63.7, (5 October 1677 in Venice – 7 March 1752 in Venice, aged 74.3), a Venetian statesman, was elected the 115th Doge of Venice, and served from this day, for 10.6 years, until his death. Grimani was a cultured and learned man, who wrote poetry, and counted among his acquaintances Isaac Newton, who he had met while serving as a diplomat in England.

28 July - Antonio Vivaldi died of "internal infection" (probably the asthmatic bronchitis from which he suffered all his life), in a house owned by the widow of a Viennese saddle maker, in poverty, in Vienna, Austria, at 63 years, 4 months and 24 days. In the same day Vivaldi was buried in a simple grave (like Mozart 50.4

years later), in a burial ground that was owned by the public hospital fund. His funeral took place at St. Stephen's Cathedral.

He is remembered as one of the greatest Baroque composers, virtuoso violinist, teacher, and cleric. His influence during his lifetime was widespread across Europe. He composed many instrumental concertos, for the violin and a variety of other instruments, as well as sacred choral works, and more than forty operas – in total over 650 compositions. Vivaldi also had some success with expensive stagings of his operas in Venice, Mantua and Vienna. His best-known work is a series of violin concertos known as "Le Quattro stagioni" ("The Four Seasons"). Vivaldi looked for harmonic contrasts and innovative melodies and themes. Many of his compositions are colorfully cheerful. Johann Sebastian Bach was deeply influenced by Vivaldi's concertos and arias (recalled in his *St John Passion*, *St Matthew Passion*, and cantatas). Bach transcribed six of Vivaldi's concerti for solo keyboard: three for organ, and one for four harpsichords, strings, and basso continuo (BWV 1065), based upon the concerto for four violins, two violas, cello, and basso continuo (RV 580).

Italia, Trieste - 22 October 2009, in Piazza del'Unita D'Italia, in Trieste, looking northeast to Palazzo del Governo.

Bach, 56, published his fourth and last *Clavier-Übung* volume, the *Goldberg Variations*, for two-manual harpsichord, contained nine canons. Throughout this period Bach also continued to adopt music of contemporaries such as Handel (born 26 days before Bach) (BNB I/K/2), and Gottfried Heinrich Stölzel (13 Jan 1690 – 27 Nov 1749, aged 59.8, prolific German baroque composer) (BWV 200), and gave many of his own earlier compositions, such as the *St Matthew* and *St John* Passions and the *Great Eighteen Chorale Preludes*, their final revisions. He also programmed and adapted music by composers of a younger generation, including Giovanni Battista Pergolesi (4 Jan 1710 – 16 March 1736, aged 26.2, Italian composer, violinist and organist; his best-known works include his Stabat Mater and the opera *La serva padrona* (*The Maid Turned Mistress*)). (BWV 1083), and his own students such as Johann Gottlieb Goldberg, 14, (12 March 1727 – 13 April 1756, aged 29.1, German virtuoso harpsichordist, organist, and composer of the late Baroque and early Classical period; he is best known for lending his name, as the probable original performer, to the renowned *Goldberg Variations* of Bach) (BNB I/G/2).

Geneva (121 BC under Romans, 375 m elevation, population 200,000, area 16 km², 70 km northwest of Mont Blanc (4810 m), 660 km southwest of Göttingen), on Rue de la Servette (to the right, going southeast, near Rue Jean Robert Chouet ((1642-1731, physician and politician) (the street is to the left, going northeast)), a nice building having down the restaurant Le Portail Chez Rui (yellow), 1.6 km northwest from Jet d'Eau, 1.6 km southwest from Palais des Nations (UN), 1.4 km northwest from the Université de Genève (1559, John Calvin (1509-1564, aged 55)).

1742 – Bach, 57, and his wife Anna, 41, had their 13th and last child, and Bach's 20th and last child, Regina Susanna Bach (1742 – 1809, aged 67).

1743 – Bach was 58 when Leopold Mozart, 24, future father of Wolfgang, was appointed as fourth violinist in the musical establishment of Count Leopold Anton von Firmian, 64, (11 March 1679 – 22 Oct 1744, aged 65.6, the ruling Prince-Archbishop of Salzburg for 17 years, from 1727 to 22 Oct 1744).

Vivaldi, Bach, Mozart, and Verdi

Germany - 23 March 1978, Freibourg im Breisgau (1120 by Duke Berthold III of Zähringen (1085-1122), elevation 278 m), from Münsterplatz looking west to the eastern main entrance and façade of Freiburger Münster (cathedral, 1200, 116 m, Johann Sebastian Bach (1685-1750) played the later versions of Passio Domini nostri J.C. secundum Evangelistam Matthæum (Matthäuspassion (St Matthew Passion)) in 1743 in this cathedral).

1744 – Bach, 59, who began to write the preludes and fugues 34 years ago, had them assembled into the second book of his monumental work *The Well-Tempered Clavier* (*Das Wohltemperierte Klavier*—"*Klavier*" meaning clavichord or harpsichord), containing 24 preludes and fugues in every major and minor key. The first book was published in 1722.

1746 – Bach, 61, was preparing to enter Lorenz Christoph Mizler von Kolof's, 35, (26 July 1711 – 8 May 1778, aged 66.8, German physician, historian, printer, mathematician, Baroque music composer) Society of Musical Sciences (1738). In order to be admitted Bach had to submit a composition, for which he chose his Canonic Variations on "Vom Himmel hoch da komm' ich her", and a portrait, which was painted by Elias Gottlob Haussmann, 51, (1695 – 11 April 1774, aged 79, German painter), and featured Bach's *Canon triplex á 6 Voc.*

1747 – May - Bach, 62, visited the court of King Frederick II, 35, (24 Jan 1712 – 17 August 1786, age 74.5, King at 28.3 for 46.2 years: 31 May 1740 – 17 August 1786) of Prussia at Potsdam. The king played a theme for Bach, and challenged him to improvise a fugue based on his theme. Bach obliged, playing a three-part fugue on one of Frederick's fortepianos, which was a new type of instrument at the time. Upon his return to Leipzig he composed a set of fugues and canons, and a trio sonata, based on the *Thema Regium* (theme of the king). Within a few weeks this music was published as *The Musical Offering*, dedicated to Frederick.

Bach entered Mizler's Society of Musical Sciences (1738).

Leopold Mozart, 28, future father of Wolfgang, married the future mother of Wolfgang, Anna Maria, 27, in Salzburg.

Italy, Venezia - The south end of La Piazzetta, the south part of Piazza San Marco, with gondole, and wedding pictures of a Japanese couple.

1748 – Bach, 63, published the *Schübler Chorales*, a set of six chorale preludes transcribed from cantata movements Bach had composed some two decades earlier. The set of five Canonic Variations, which Bach had submitted when entering Mizler's Society in 1747, was also printed.

1749 – January – Bach was 63.8 when his daughter Elisabeth Juliane Friederica, 23, (1726 – 1781, aged 55, called Liesgen), married his pupil Johann Christoph Altnickol, 29, (1 Jan 1720 – 25 July 1759, aged 39.5, German organist, bass singer, and composer).

6 April - Antonio Schinella Conti died in Padua, aged 72.2 (22 Jan 1677, Padua – 6 April 1749), also known by his religious title as Abate Conti, was an Italian mathematician, writer, translator, philosopher and physicist. He was an older contemporaneous Italian with Vivaldi (Conti was 1.1 years older than Vivaldi, and died 7.8 years after him).

1750 – March and April – Bach, 65, becoming blind, underwent unsuccessful eye surgery from the British self-promoted eye surgeon John Taylor, 47, (1703 – 1772, aged 69).

28 July - Johann Sebastian Bach died in Leipzig (31 March 1685 in Eisenach – 28 July 1750, aged 65 years, 3 months and 28 days, of complications after eye surgery). He has been generally regarded as one of the greatest composers of all time, and also one of the greatest fathers, with 20 children. At Bach's death his second wife Anna was 48.8, and the remaining 9 children were: Catharina 42, Wilhelm 40, Carl 36, Gottfried 26, Elisabeth 24, Christoph 18, Christian 15, Johanna 13, and Regina 8.

Paris - On the façade of l'Opéra de Paris (1875): a statue and the bust of Johann Sebastian Bach (1685 – 1750), one of the greatest German composers and organists, who wrote the Branderburg Concertos, the Well-Tempered Clavier, over 200 cantatas, Passions, and keyboard works. Mozart, Beethoven, Chopin, Schumann and Mendelssohn were admirers of Bach. Beethoven described him as the "Urvater der Harmonie" (the original father of harmony).

1751– 17 January - Tomaso Albinoni died (8 June 1671, in Venezia – 17 January 1751, aged 79.5) He was an older contemporaneous Italian Baroque composer with Vivaldi and Bach (Albinoni was born 6.7 years before Vivaldi, and 13.8 years before Bach, then Albinoni died 9.5 years after Vivaldi, and almost half a year after Bach).

Bach's son Carl Philipp Emanuel, 37, saw to it that Bach's *The Art of Fugue*, although still unfinished, was published.

1754 – 23 August: in Palace of Versailles, France, the grandson of current King of France Louis XV (44 years old), Louis-Auguste was born – almost 20 years later he will become King Louis XVI.

1755 – 11 Feb -Francesco Scipione, marchese di Maffei, or Scipione Maffei died in Verona, aged 79.7 (1 June 1675, Verona – 11 Feb 1755, Italian writer and art critic, author of many articles and plays).

Chapter 2. Wolfgang Amadeus Mozart

1756 – 27 January – Wolfgang Amadeus Mozart was born (27 January 1756, at 9 Getreidegasse, Salzburg (423 m elevation, 250 km east of Vienna, 270 km north of Venezia, ecclesiastic principality part of the Holy Roman Empire, now Austria) – 5 December 1791, Vienna, Austria, aged 35 years, 10 months and 8 days). He was baptized the day after his birth, at St. Rupert's Cathedral in Salzburg, as Johannes Chrysostomus Wolfgangus Theophilus Mozart, and was a prolific and influential composer of the classical era. Mozart showed prodigious ability from his earliest childhood. He was the son of a court musician for Sigismund Graf von Schrattenbach, 58, (28 February 1698 – 16 December 1771, aged 73.8) who was Prince-Archbishop of Salzburg for 18 years, from 1753 to 1771), and reputable violin teacher (he published in 1756 a violin textbook, *Versuch einer gründlichen Violinschule*, which achieved success), Leopold Mozart, 37, (1719, Augburg, Germany – 1787, aged 68) and Anna Maria Mozart, 36, (1720 – 1778, aged 58). He was the youngest of seven children, five of whom died in infancy, remaining only him and his sister. His elder sister was Maria Anna Mozart, 5, (1751–1829, aged 78), nicknamed "Nannerl".

1757 – 23 July - Domenico Scarlatti died in Madrid (26 Oct 1685 – 23 July 1757, aged 71.7), son of Alessandro Scarlatti (2 May 1660 – 22 Oct 1725, aged 65.4).

1759 – 14 April - George Frideric Handel died in London (5 March 1685 – 14 April 1759, aged 74.1, burial place Westminster Abbey, London).

Wolfgang, 3, learned to play clavier, when his older sister Nannerl, 8, began keyboard lessons with their father, who also taught his children languages and academic subjects.

London - From the Broad Sanctuary, west of St. Margaret's Church, looking southwest to the west part of the north façade (north entrance (left)) of Westminster Abbey (960, 1517, Collegiate Church of St. Peter at Westminster, Anglican abbey hosting daily services, and every coronation since 1066, tower height 69 m, floor area 3,000 m^2).

1760 – Mozart, 4, wrote his first melody.

25 Oct: King George II (George Augustus) died, and the new King is his grandson George III (1738-1820 (aged 81.6), king 1760 (22.3) – 1820 (for 59 years and 3 months king), had 15 children).

1761 – Mozart was only 5 years old when he first played publicly, as a keyboards performer. He was already recognized as a child prodigy.

1762 – 17 Sep - Francesco Saverio Geminiani died in Dublin, Ireland, aged 74.8 (5 Dec 1687, Lucca, Italy – 17 Sep 1762, Italian violinist, composer, and music theorist).
Mozart, 6, teaches himself to play violin, and with his father, 43, and his older sister Nannerl, 11, travel to Munich and Vienna, performing as prodigies at the court of Prince-elector Maximilian III

Joseph, 35, (28 March 1727 – 30 Dec 1777, aged 50.7) of Bavaria in Munich, and at the Imperial Courts in Vienna and Prague.

<u>1763 - 1766</u>– Leopold Mozart, 44, who became the orchestra's deputy Kapellmeister in 1763, for Sigismund Graf von Schrattenbach, 65, (28 February 1698 – 16 December 1771, aged 73.8) who was Prince-Archbishop of Salzburg for 18 years, from 1753 to 1771), takes his two children, 12 and 7 years old, to a long concert tour, spanning three and a half years, taking the family to the courts of Munich, Mannheim, Paris, London, The Hague, again to Paris, and back home via Zurich, Donaueschingen, and Munich.[1] During this trip, Wolfgang met a number of musicians and acquainted himself with the works of other composers from Germany, Belgium, France and England. Young Wolfgang, 7, begins to compose his first pieces.

<u>1764</u> – Mozart, 8, received important influence regarding the concerto style from Johann Christian Bach, 29, (5 Sep 1735 – 1 Jan 1782, aged 46.3, J. S. Bach's 18th child, and youngest son), whom he visited in London in 1764 and 1765.

Mozart wrote his first symphony in Sol-flat when he was eight years old, and it is probable that his father transcribed most of it for him. In the summer the father was sick.

London - From the Abingdon St., looking northeast to the south (left, House of Commons) and west (right, House of Lords) façades of the Palace of Westminster, with the Old Palace Yard, and the statue of the King Richard I of England (Coeur de Lion (the Lionheart), 1157-1199, King 1189-1199, center).

1765 – Michel Corrette (10 April 1707 – 21 Jan 1795, aged 87.8, French organist, composer, and author of musical method books) based his motet Laudate Dominum de coelis on Vivaldi's Primavera (Spring) from Le Quattro Stagioni.

Autumn – in Hague, Mozart, 9, and his sister, 14, were sick.

Beaumarchais, 33, wrote the well-known Figaro plays Le Barbier de Séville, and Le Mariage de Figaro, inspired from his travels in Spain in 1764, and first appeared in Le Sacristain.

1766 – Mozart, 10, was sick from smallpox.

1767 – 25 June - Georg Philipp Telemann died at 86 years 3 months and 1 day (24 March 1681 – 25 June 1767, German Baroque composer and multi-instrumentalist).

The Mozart family again went to Vienna in late 1767, and remained there for about one year, until December 1768.

1768 – Mozart, 12, writes in Vienna his first opera "La finta semplice", and a Mass.

1769 - 15 August: Napoleone di Buonaparte was born in Corsica.

December - After one year in Salzburg, Leopold, 50, and Wolfgang, 13, set off for Italy, leaving mother Anna Maria, 49, and sister Nannerl, 17, at home. This tour lasted from December 1769 to March 1771.

Italy, 6 April 1978, Pisa, Palazzo della Carovana (1562-1564) now for Scuola Normale Superiore (1810, by Napoleon Bonaparte (1769-1821), 460 students, 6% admission rate, best in Italy).

1770 – Wolfgang, 14, met Josef Mysliveček, 33, (9 March 1737 – 4 Feb 1781, aged 43.9, Czech composer) and Giovanni Battista Martini, 64, (24 April 1706 – 3 August 1784, aged 78.3, also known as Padre Martini, Italian musician and composer) in Bologna, and was accepted as a member of the famous Accademia Filarmonica di Bologna (1666). In Rome, he received from Pope Clement XIV, 65, (31 Oct 1705 – 22 Sep 1774, aged 68.9, Pope for 5.3 years (19 May 1769 – 22 Sep 1774)) the badge of the Order of the Golden Spur. Then he heard Gregorio Allegri's (c. 1582 – 7 Feb 1652, aged 70, Italian priest and composer) *Miserere* twice in performance, in the Sistine Chapel, and wrote it out from memory, thus producing the first unauthorized copy of this closely guarded property of the Vatican.

In Milan, Mozart wrote the opera *Mitridate, re di Ponto* (1770), which was performed with success. This led to further opera commissions.

17 December – Mozart was 14.9 when Ludwig von Beethoven was born (17 Dec 1770 – 26 March 1827, aged 56 years, 3 months and 9 days).

1771 – August – December: Wolfgang, 15.5, returned with his father to Milano, for the composition and premiere of *Ascanio in Alba*.

1772 – October – 13 March 1773: Wolfgang, 16.7, returned with his father to Milano, for the composition and premiere of Lucio Silla. The father Leopold hoped that these visits would result in a professional appointment for his son, and indeed ruling Archduke Ferdinand, 18, (1 June 1754, Schönbrunn Palace, Vienna, Austria, Holy Roman Empire – 24 Dec 1806, Vienna, Austrian Empire, aged 52.6) contemplated hiring Mozart (1.3 years younger), but his mother Empress Maria Theresa, 55, (13 May 1717 – 29 Nov 1780, aged 63.5) did not agree, and the matter was dropped.

1773 – February – Mozart, 17, in Italy with his father, 54, wrote the work, which is still widely performed today, the solo motet *Exsultate, jubilate*, K. 165.

13 March – Mozart, 17.1, and his father returned from Italy, and he was engaged as a court musician (150 florins (about $21,000)/year) by the ruler of Salzburg, Prince-Archbishop Hieronymus von Colloredo, 40.8, (31 May 1732, Vienna, Austria, Holy Roman Empire – 20 May 1812, Vienna, Austrian Empire, aged 79.9 (11 days before 80), installed on 22 June 1772 – archbishopric abolished in 1803). Mozart worked on symphonies, sonatas, string quartets, masses, serenades, and a few minor operas, but he wanted to find another place to work.

14 July – 26 September: Mozart and his father visited Vienna.

16 Dec: the Boston Tea Party protest takes place, in which 342 chests of tea belonging to the British East India Company were thrown from ships into Boston Harbor, by American patriots disguised as Mohawk Indians. A Virginia committee of correspondence was formed to communicate with other colonies.

USA, Boston Harbor (founded in 1630), in 2009: visiting tall ships from many countries, at the Boston Fish Pier (opened in 1915).

1774 – 10 May: King of France Louis XV died at 64.2.

The new King of France was his grandson Louis XVI (23 Aug 1754 – 21 Jan 1793 (aged 38.4), King 10 May 1774 (age 19.7) – 30 Sep 1792 (age 38), for 8.3 years).

6 Dec – March 1775: Mozart, 18.9, and his father, 55, visited Munich, where he had a popular success with the premiere of his opera *La finta giardiniera*.

1775 – Jean-Jacques Rousseau (28 June 1712, Geneva, Switzerland – 2 July 1778, Ermenonville, France, aged 65.9, 4 days before 66, Genevan philosopher, writer, and composer of the 18th century, mainly active in France. Quotes: Man is born free, and everywhere he is in chains. What wisdom can you find that is greater than kindness?), reworked Vivaldi's Primavera (Spring) from Le Quattro Stagioni, into a version for solo flute.

19 April: American minutemen at Lexington and Concord, in Massachusetts, clash with British troops.

April – December: Mozart, 19, in Salzburg, worked with enthusiasm on violin concertos, producing a series of five (the only ones he ever wrote). The last three—K. 216, K. 218, K. 219—are now frequently in the repertoire.

The Salzburg court theatre was closed, and Mozart wanted to compose operas.

1776 – 17 March: after 8 months of fighting, British troops, under General Sir William Howe, evacuated Boston, leaving 200 cannons and stores of small arms and munitions, and the first phase of Washington's (44) command was successful.

4th of July: the United States Declaration of Independence (Thomas Jefferson (33, Virginia) was the principal author, with Benjamin Franklin (70, Pennsylvania) and John Adams (40.7, Massachusetts)) was adopted by the Second Continental Congress meeting at the Pennsylvania State House (Independence Hall) in Philadelphia, which announced that the thirteen American colonies, then at war with the Kingdom of Great Britain, regarded themselves as thirteen independent sovereign states, no longer under British rule. It was signed by 56 signers.

Mozart, 20, in Salzburg, works on piano concertos.

Boston, USA - 11 July 2009, at the northwest end of Boston Fish Pier, northwest of the Exchange Conference Center (right) a Lexington Minutemen (armed volunteers ready to go in a minute) unit in 1776 uniforms.

1777 – January - Mozart, 21, in Salzburg, wrote the piano concerto number 9 "Jenamy" (for the pianist Victoire Jenamy) in Mi bemolle maggiore K 271, which is exceptional.

August – Mozart, 21.6, resigned his position at Salzburg court.

23 September – Mozart started again his search of employment, with visits to Augsburg, Mannheim, Paris, and Munich. In Mannheim Mozart became acquainted with members of its famous orchestra, the best in Europe at the time. He also fell in love with Aloysia Weber, 17, (c. 1760 – 8 June 1839, aged 79, German soprano), one of four daughters of the musical family Weber.

1778 – 14 March – Mozart, 22, left for Paris, to continue his search of employment. He stayed with Friedrich Melchior, Baron von Grimm, 54.2, (26 December 1723 – 19 December 1807, aged

83.9 (7 days before 84), German-born French-language journalist, art critic, diplomat, and, as personal secretary of Louis Philippe I, Duke d'Orléans, 52.8, (12 May 1725 – 18 November 1785, aged 60.5, French prince, a member of a cadet branch of the House of Bourbon, the dynasty then ruling France), lived in his mansion).

12 June – Mozart's La minor piano sonata number 8, K.310/300d was performed in Paris.

18 June – Mozart's "Paris" Symphony (Number 31) was performed in Paris.

2 July - Jean-Jacques Rousseau (who was good friend with Friedrich Melchior, Baron von Grimm) died in Ermenonville, France, aged 65.9, 4 days before 66 (28 June 1712, Geneva, Switzerland – 2 July 1778, Genevan philosopher, writer, and composer).

3 July - Mozart's mother Anna Maria Mozart died at 58 (1720 – 1778).

Mozart, in Paris, with the help of his father, 59, from Salzburg, was offered a post as Salzburg court organist and concertmaster, with the annual salary of 450 florins ($63,000).

3 August – Teatro alla Scala was inaugurated in Milano, Italia.

Italy, 20 April 1978, Milano, in Piazza della Scala (Largo Antonio Ghiringhelli (1906-1979, left), looking northwest to the southeast façade of Teatro alla Scala (3 August 1778, capacity 2,800).

September – Mozart left Paris for Salzburg, passing by Mannheim and Munich. In Munich, he again encountered Aloysia, 18, now a very successful singer, but she was no longer interested in him.

The east side of l'Opéra de Paris (or l'Opéra Garnier, 1875), a 1,979-seat opera house, seen from Rue Halévy and Rue Glück.

1779 – 15 January – Mozart, almost 23, returned to Salzburg, and took up his new appointment at the court, but his discontentment with Salzburg remained.

1780 – Mozart, 24, worked on his opera Idomeneo.

1781 – January - Mozart, 25, had his opera *Idomeneo* premiered with "considerable success" in Munich.

16 March – Mozart was called from Salzburg to Vienna, where his employer, Archbishop Colloredo, 49, was attending the celebrations for the accession of Joseph II, 40, (13 March 1741 – 20 Feb 1790, aged 48.9 (21 days before 49)) to the Hungary, Croatia and Bohemia throne, while he was King of the Romans, Holy Roman Emperor, and Archduke of Austria.

May - Mozart attempted to resign, and was refused by Archbishop Colloredo.

Because of the disputes with his employer Archbishop Colloredo, Mozart moved in with the Weber family, who had moved to Vienna from Mannheim. The father, Fridolin, had died, and the

Webers were now taking in lodgers to make some money. Aloysia, 21, who had earlier rejected Mozart's suit, was now married (from 31 Oct 1780) to the actor and artist Joseph Lange, 30, (1 April 1751 – 17 Sep 1831, aged 80.5, actor and amateur painter). Mozart fell in love with the third Weber daughter, Constanze Weber, 19.3, (5 Jan 1762 – 6 March 1842, aged 80.1, trained as a singer). Constanze had two older sisters, Josepha and Aloysia, and one younger one, Sophie (1763 – 1846, aged 83). A paternal half-cousin of Constanze was Carl Maria von Weber (18 Nov 1786 – 5 June 1826, aged 39.5, German composer, conductor, pianist, guitarist and critic).

June – Mozart received the permission to resign from Archbishop Colloredo's court, in an uncivilized way.

He chose to stay in the capital, as a freelance performer and composer.

5 September – Because Constanze's mother Cäcilia Weber noticed that Mozart was courting Constanze, and in the interest of propriety, the mother requested that he leave. Mozart moved out to a third-floor room in the Graben.

24 December – Mozart, 25.9, performed in a competition, before the Emperor Joseph II, with Muzio Clementi, 29.9, (23 Jan 1752 – 10 March 1832, aged 80.1, buried at Westminster Abbey, Italian-born English composer, pianist, pedagogue, conductor, music publisher, editor, and piano manufacturer).

London - Detail of the north entrance of Westminster Abbey (960, 1517, Collegiate Church of St Peter at Westminster, Anglican abbey hosting daily services, and every coronation since 1066, tower height 69 m, floor area 3,000 m^2).

1782 – 10 April – Mozart, 26.2, wrote to his father Leopold, 63: "I go every Sunday at twelve o'clock to the Baron van Swieten, where nothing is played but Handel and Bach. I am collecting at the moment the fugues of Bach—not only of Sebastian, but also of Emanuel and Friedemann." At that time, Bach's younger son Emanuel was 68 years old, and older son Friedemann was 71.5 years old. In this way, Mozart began to study the work of Johann Sebastian Bach and George Frideric Handel, as a result of the influence of the Baron Gottfried van Swieten, 49, (29 Oct 1733 – 29 March 1803, in Vienna, aged 69.4, diplomat, librarian, government official who served the Austrian Empire, enthusiastic amateur musician, and the patron of several great composers of the Classical era, including Joseph Haydn, Wolfgang Amadeus Mozart, and Ludwig van Beethoven), who owned many manuscripts of the Baroque masters. Mozart's study of these scores inspired compositions in Baroque style, and later influenced his personal musical language, for example in fugal passages in *Die Zauberflöte* ("The Magic Flute", 1791) and the finale of Symphony No. 41.[1]

16 July - Mozart, 26.5, had the premier of his opera *Die Entführung aus dem Serail* ("The Abduction from the Seraglio"), which had a great success.

4 August – Mozart, 26.6, married Constance Webber, 20.6, in St. Stephen's Cathedral, the day before his father's consent arrived in the mail. They had six children, of whom only two survived infancy.

Italy, Venezia - Libreria Sansoviniana (left), Il Campanile (center-left), Palazzo Ducale (right), and a Japanese couple wedding picture.

1783 – Spring: Mozart, 27, and his wife Constanze, 21, visited his family in Salzburg. His father, 64, and sister Nannerl, 32, were cordially polite to Constanze, and the visit prompted the composition of one of Mozart's great liturgical pieces, the Great Mass in do minor K 427, missa solemnis. Though not completed, it was premiered in Salzburg, with Constanze singing a solo part

17 June – Mozart, 27.4, and his wife Constanze, 21.4, had their first child Raimund Leopold (17 June – 19 August 1783, 2 months).

Sunday 26 October – Mozart's Great Mass in do minor K 427, missa solemnis, though not completed, it was premiered in the Church of St. Peter's Abbey in Salzburg, with Constanze singing the solo part "Et incarnatus est".

1784 – Mozart, 28, met Joseph Haydn, 52, in Vienna around 1784, and the two composers became friends. When Haydn visited Vienna, they sometimes played together in an impromptu string quartet. Mozart's six quartets dedicated to Haydn (K. 387, K. 421, K. 428, K. 458, K. 464, and K. 465) date from the period 1782 to 1785, and are judged to be a response to Haydn's Opus 33 set from 1781.

21 September - Mozart, 28.7, and his wife Constanze, 22.7, had their second child Karl Thomas Mozart (21 September 1784, Vienna – 31 October 1858, Milano, Italy, aged 74.1, pianist, but worked as an official in the service of the Austrian financial administration and the governmental accounting department in Milan. He also served as official translator for Italian for the Austrian Court Chamber. Like his younger brother, he neither married nor had children, and the direct Mozart line thus died with him).

14 December - Mozart became a Freemason (member of one of the fraternal organizations that trace their origins to the local fraternities of stonemasons), admitted to the lodge Zur Wohltätigkeit ("Beneficence"). He composed Masonic music, e.g. the Maurerische Trauermusik.

1785 – Mozart, 29, had, from 1782 to 1785, mounted concerts with himself as soloist, presenting three or four new piano concertos in each season. He booked a large room in the Trattnerhof (an apartment building), and the ballroom of the Mehlgrube (a restaurant). The concerts were and still are very popular. With sizeable returns from his concerts and elsewhere, Mozart and his wife, 23, adopted a rather rich lifestyle. They moved to an expensive apartment, with a yearly rent of 460 florins ($64,400). Mozart bought a fine fortepiano (today on display in the main hall of the

Tanzmeisterhaus, where the Mozart family lived in Salzburg after 1773; the location is now a Mozart museum) from Anton Walter, 33, (5 Feb 1752 – 11 April 1826, aged 74.1, the most famous Viennese piano maker of his time) for about 900 florins ($126,000), and a billiard table for about 300 ($42,000). The Mozarts sent their son Karl Thomas (1 year old) to an expensive boarding school, and kept servants. Saving was therefore difficult, and the short period of financial success did nothing to soften the hardship the Mozarts were later to experience.

November – Mozart, 29.8 began his operatic collaboration with the librettist Lorenzo Da Ponte, 36.6, (10 March 1749 – 17 August 1838, aged 89.4, Italian, later American opera librettist, poet and Roman Catholic priest. He wrote the libretti for 28 operas by 11 composers, including three of Mozart's greatest operas, *The Marriage of Figaro, Don Giovanni*, and *Così fan tutte).*

Paris - The central part of the façade of L'Opéra de Paris (1875): composers Daniel Auber (1782–1871, left), Ludwig van Beethoven (1770–1827, second), Wolfgang Amadeus Mozart (1756–1791, center) and Gaspare Spontini (1774–1851, right).

1786 – 1 May - Mozart, 30.3, had the successful premiere of his opera, with him as conductor, "Le nozze di Figaro" ("The Marriage of Figaro") at Burgtheater in Vienna, librettist Lorenzo Da Ponte, based on the stage comedy "La folle journée, ou le Mariage de Figaro" by Pierre Beaumarchais (performed two years earlier, in 1784). Its reception in Prague later in the year was even warmer.

18 October - Mozart, 30.7, and his wife Constanze, 24.7, had their third child Johann Thomas Leopold (18 October – 15 November 1786, 27 days).

18 November - Carl Maria von Weber was born (18 Nov 1786 – 5 June 1826, aged 39.5, German composer, conductor, pianist, guitarist and critic). He was a paternal half-cousin of Constanze Mozart.

December - Mozart appeared less frequently in public concerts, and his income shrank.

1787 –28 May - Mozart's (31.3) father Leopold, who helped his son all the time, died at 68.

The young Ludwig van Beethoven, 16.5, spent several weeks in Vienna, and probably studied with Mozart, but no reliable records survive to indicate whether the two composers ever met.

29 October – Mozart's (31.8) opera *Don Giovanni* premiered, with him as conductor, to acclaim at Estates Theatre in Prague.

15 November - Christoph Willibald (Ritter von) Gluck died at 73.3 (2 July 1714 – 15 Nov 1787, composer of Italian and French opera).

December - Mozart obtained a steady post under aristocratic patronage. Emperor Joseph II, 46.6, appointed him as his "chamber composer", a post that had fallen vacant on 15 Nov on the death of Christoph Willibald (Ritter von) Gluck. It was a part-time appointment, paying 800 florins ($112,000) per year, and required Mozart only to compose dances for the annual balls in the Redoutensaal.

27 December - Mozart, 31.9, and his wife Constanze, 25.9, had their fourth child Theresia Constanzia Adelheid Friedericke Maria Anna (27 December 1787 – 29 June 1788, 6 months).

Switzerland, Geneva, from Quai Gustave Ador (1845-1928, President). Jet d'Eau (1886, 1891, 1951) – a large fountain pumping lake water at 500 liters/s to 140 m, lit up at night. It is located at the point where Lac Léman empties into the Rhône River. There are two 500 kW pumps, operating at 2,400 V, consuming one megawatt of electricity. The water leaves the nozzle (10.16 cm) at a speed of 200 km/h. At any time, there are about 7,000 liters of water in the air.

1788 – February – The Austro-Turkish War begins; it was fought for 3.5 years, until 4 August 1791, between the Habsburg Monarchy (Austria) and the Ottoman Empire, concurrently with the Russo-Turkish War (1787–1792, 5 years). It is sometimes referred to as the Habsburg–Ottoman War or the Austro-Ottoman War.

7 May - Mozart's (32.3) opera *Don Giovanni* premiered, with him as conductor, in Vienna, with Donna Anna being played by soprano Aloysia Weber, 28, an older sister of Constanze, 26.3.

July - Mozart and his family had moved from central Vienna to the suburb of Alsergrund, for more housing space. Mozart began to borrow money (while living comfortable, and also owning a carriage and a horse), most often from his friend and fellow Mason Michael von Puchberg, 47, (21 Sep 1741 – 21 Jan 1822, aged 80 years and 4 months, textile merchant who lived in Vienna, lent about 1400 florins ($200,000) to Mozart, paid back by Constanze, a few years after her husband died).

Major works of this year include the last three symphonies (Numbers 39, 40, and 41).

1789 – Spring: Mozart, 33, made some long journeys, hoping to improve his finances, to Leipzig (450 km northwest of Vienna), Dresden (in April, 100 km southeast of Leipzig), and Berlin (170 km north of Dresden, and 530 km northwest of Vienna).

16 November - Mozart, 33.8, and his wife Constanze, 27.8, had their fifth child Anna Maria (died soon after birth, 16 November 1789).

1790– 26 January - Mozart, one day before his 34th birthday, had the premiere, with him as conductor, at Burgtheater in Vienna, of his Italian opera buffa "Cosi fan Tutte", librettist Lorenzo Da Ponte.

20 February – Emperor Joseph II died at 48.9 (13 March 1741 – 20 Feb 1790).

Leopold II, 42.8, (5 May 1747 – 1 March 1792, aged 44.8) became the new Emperor for 2 years.

Mozart again made some long journeys, hoping to improve his finances, to Frankfurt (600 km northwest of Vienna), Mannheim

(80 km south of Frankfurt), and other German cities. Not much financial improvements.

1791– 5 January - Mozart, 34.9, composed the final piano concerto number 27 (K. 595 in Si bemol major (B♭)).

4 March – Mozart's piano concerto number 27 (K. 595 in Si bemol major (B♭)) was performed, with him, in Vienna.

He also composed the Clarinet Concerto K.622; the last in his great series of string quintets (K. 614 in Mi bemol major (E♭)); the motet Ave verum corpus K. 618; and the unfinished Requiem K. 626. Mozart no longer borrowed large sums from Puchberg, and made a start on paying off his debts.

26 July - Mozart, 35.5, and his wife Constanze, 29.5, had their sixth child Franz Xaver Wolfgang Mozart (26 July 1791 – 29 July 1844, aged 53 years and 3 days, composer, pianist, conductor, and teacher, whose musical style was heavily influenced by his father's mature style; he neither married nor had children).

6 September – Mozart had the premier, with him as conductor, at the Estates Theatre in Prague, of his Italian opera seria *La clemenza di Tito,* Italian libretto by Caterino Mazzolà, 46.6, (18 Jan 1745 – 16 July 1806, Venezia, aged 61.5, Italian poet and librettist), after Pietro Metastasio (3 Jan 1698, Roma, Papal States – 12 April 1782, Vienna, Holy Roman Empire, aged 84.2, Italian poet and librettist, considered the most important writer of *opera seria* libretti). This opera is about the Roman emperor Titus Flavius Vespasianus (30 Dec 39 – 13 Sep 81, aged 41.7, emperor for 2.2 years, from 23 June 79 (aged 39.5) to 13 Sep 81). Mozart composed this opera during this year, on commission for the Emperor Leopold II 's coronation festivities.

Italy, Roma - Arco di Tito (Arch of Titus, 82 AD, restored in 1821, left), and the church Santa Francesca Romana (975 – 1615, right).

Mozart fell ill while in Prague (250 km northwest of Vienna).

30 September – Mozart had the premier, with him as conductor, at Schikaneder's theatre, the Freihaus-Theater auf der Wieden in Vienna, of his German opera in the form of a Singspiel (singing and spoken dialog) *Die Zauberflöte* ("The Magic Flute"), German libretto by Emanuel Schikaneder, 40, (1 Sep 1751 – 21 Sep 1812, aged 61, German impresario, dramatist, actor, singer and composer; he played the role of Papageno)).

17 November – Mozart's Little Masonic Cantata K. 623, was premiered.

20 November – Mozart's health deteriorated, at which point he became bedridden, suffering from swelling, pain, fever, etc.

Mozart was nursed in his final illness by his wife, and her youngest sister Sophie, 28, and was attended by the family doctor, Thomas Franz Closset. He was mentally occupied with the task of finishing his Requiem, but there is no much evidence that he actually dictated passages to his student Franz Xaver Süssmayr, 25, (1766 –

17 Sep 1803, aged 37, Austrian composer and conductor, who, upon Constanze's request, completed Mozart's unfinished Requiem within 100 days of Mozart's death).

5 December at 12:55 AM in the night - Wolfgang Amadeus Mozart died in his home, probably because of a streptococcal infection (the official record wrote *hitziges Frieselfieber* ("severe miliary fever", referring to a rash that looks like millet seeds)), aged 35 years, 10 months and 8 days (27 January 1756 – 5 December 1791). His wife Constanze was 29.9, his older son Karl was 7.1 years old, and his younger son Franz was 4 months old.

Baron Gottfried van Swieten, 58.1, showed up at his home and made the funeral arrangements. He may have temporarily helped support the surviving Mozarts, as Constanze's correspondence in several places mentions his "generosity".

7 December - Mozart was interred in an individual grave, as it was the Viennese custom, at the St. Marx Cemetery, outside the city. It is probable that Antonio Salieri, 41, (18 August – 1750 – 7 May 1825, aged 74.7, Italian classical composer, conductor, and teacher, born in Legnago, south of Verona, in the Republic of Venice, and spent his adult life and career as a subject of the Habsburg Monarchy in Vienna), Süssmayr, 25, van Swieten, 58, and two other musicians were present.

In the period immediately after Mozart's death, his reputation rose considerably.

Mozart composed more than 600 works, many acknowledged as pinnacles of symphonic, concertante, chamber, operatic, and choral music. He is among the most enduringly popular of classical composers, and his influence is profound on subsequent music. Ludwig van Beethoven composed his own early works in the shadow of Mozart, and Joseph Haydn wrote very nice about him.

1792 – 29 February - Gioachino Rossini was born (29 February 1792 – 13 November 1868, aged 76.7, Italian composer who wrote 39 operas, as well as some sacred music, songs, chamber music, and piano pieces; he was a precocious composer of operas, and he made his debut at age 18).

15 March - Franz Xaver Süssmayr, 26, upon Constanze's request, completed Mozart's unfinished Requiem, and returned it to Constanze.

1793 – 2 January - Baron Gottfried van Swieten, 59.2, sponsored a performance of Mozart's *Requiem* as a benefit concert for Constanze, 31; it yielded a profit of 300 ducats, a substantial sum. He was also reported to have helped arrange for the education of Mozart's son Karl, 8.2, in Prague.

1797 – 29 November - Gaetano Donizetti was born (29 November 1797 – 8 April 1848, aged 50.4, Italian composer).

1801 – 3 November - Vincenzo Bellini was born (3 November 1801 – 23 September 1835, aged 33.9, Italian opera composer).

1804 – 18 May - Napoléon Bonaparte, 34.7, becomes the Emperor of the French, until 6 April 1814.

1805 – 17 March - Napoléon Bonaparte, 35.6, becomes the King of Italy, until 11 April 1814.
26 May - Napoléon Bonaparte, 35.7, has the Coronation, at the Milan Cathedral, as the King of Italy, until 11 April 1814.

Oxford: From Merton Str., looking southeast to the north (left) and west (right) facades of Merton College Chapel (1294, 1425, 1451, the church of Merton College (1264, the third oldest in Oxford)); there were plans to extend this church to the west (right), but the land was leased in 1517 to Bishop Richard Foxe (1448-1528), who founded Corpus Christy College (1517), next door (west) to Merton.

1806 – 10 August - Michael Haydn, the younger brother of Joseph Haydn, died (14 Sep 1737 – 10 August 1806, aged 68.9).

1808 – Napoléon Bonaparte, 39, Emperor of the French and King of Italy, annexed the Duchy of Parma and Piacenza from Italy to the First French Empire.

1809 – 31 May - Joseph Haydn died (31 March 1732 – 31 May 1809, aged 77 years and 2 months, an Austrian composer of the Classical period. He was a contemporaneous friend and mentor of Mozart (27 January 1756 – 5 December 1791, aged 35 years, 10 months and 8 days; Haydn was born 23.9 years before Mozart, and died 17.4 years after Mozart), a teacher of Beethoven (17 Dec 1770 – 26 March 1827, aged 56 years, 3 months and 9 days), and the older brother of composer Michael Haydn (14 Sep 1737 – 10 August 1806, aged 68.9; Joseph was born 5.5 years before Michael, and died 2.7 years after him; Michael Haydn also was a contemporaneous composer of Mozart (Michael was born 18.3 years before Mozart, and died 14.6 years after him)).

Chapter 3. Giuseppe Verdi

1813 – 9 October – Giuseppe Verdi was born at family's home, the first child of Carlo Giuseppe Verdi, 28, (1785 – 1867, aged 82, innkeeper) and Luigia Uttini Verdi, 26, (1787 – 1851, aged 64, spinner), in Le Roncole (90 km southeast of Milano, 90 km southwest of Verona, and 400 km northwest of Roma), a village 4 km southeast of Busseto, then in the Département Taro, which was a part of the First French Empire under Napoléon Bonaparte, 44.1, (15 August 1769 – 5 May 1821, aged 51.7, Emperor of the French 18 May 1804 – 6 April 1814, King of Italy 17 March 1805 – 11 April 1814, Coronation on 26 May 1805 at Milan Cathedral), after the annexation of the Duchy of Parma and Piacenza in 1808. Verdi full name was Giuseppe Fortunino Francesco Verdi. He was born to a provincial family of moderate means, and developed a musical education with the help of a local patron.

Italia, Milano - 30 Sep 2008, in Piazza del Duomo, looking southeast to the north side of il Duomo (Basilica Cattedrale metropolitana di Santa Maria Nascente, 1386-1965 (579 years), capacity 40,000, length 158.5 m, width 92 m, maximum height 108 m, 135 spires, materials: brick and Candoglia marble, architects: Donato Bramante (1444-1514), Leonardo da Vinci (1452-1519), Giulio Romano (1499-1546), Pellegrino Tibaldi (1527-1596)). On May 20, 1805, Napoleon Bonaparte (1769-1821), about to be crowned King of Italy, ordered the façade to be finished by Pellicani. For this, a statue of Napoleon was placed at the top of one of the spires. Napoleon was crowned King of Italy at the Duomo on May 26, 1805.

11 October – Giuseppe was baptized, and the baptismal register lists Verdi as being "born yesterday", but since days were often considered to begin at sunset, this could have meant either 9 or 10 October. Following his mother, Verdi always celebrated his birthday on 9 October, the day he himself believed he was born.

1814 – 6 April – Giuseppe was 5.9 months old when Napoléon Bonaparte, 44.6, ended his reign as the Emperor of the French.

11 April – Giuseppe was 6 months old when Napoléon Bonaparte, 44.6, ended his reign as the King of Italy.

4 May – Margherita Barezzi was born (4 May 1814 – 18 June 1840, aged 36.1, Verdi's wife 1836 – 1840; Verdi was 6 months and 25 days older than Margherita).

1815 – 8 Sep – Verdi was 1 year and 11 months when Giuseppina Strepponi was born (8 Sep 1815 – 14 Nov 1897, aged 82.2, operatic soprano of great renown).

1816 – Giuseppe's younger sister Giuseppa was born (1816 – 1833, aged 17).

1817 – Giuseppe, 4, was given private lessons in Latin and Italian, by the village schoolmaster, Baistrocchi.

1819 – Giuseppe, 6, attended the local school, and began learning to play the organ.

1820 – Giuseppe, 7, showed so much interest in music that his father finally provided him with a spinet (small piano).

Verdi's gift for music was already apparent by the end of this year, when he, with the help of his father, began his association with the local church, serving in the choir, acting as an altar boy for a while, and taking organ lessons.

1821 – 5 May   Giuseppe was 7.6 years old when Napoléon Bonaparte died on St Helen Island (15 August 1769 – 5 May 1821, aged 51.7).

After Baistrocchi's death, Verdi, at the age of eight, with the help of his father, became the official paid organist.

1823 – Verdi, 10, was enroll by his father to attend school in Busseto, enrolling him in a *Ginnasio* — an upper school for boys — run by Don Pietro Seletti, while the parents continued to run their inn at Le Roncole.

Verdi returned to Busseto regularly to play the organ on Sundays, covering the distance of 4 km each way on foot.

1824 – Verdi, 11, received schooling in Italian, Latin, the humanities, and rhetoric.

He also began lessons with Ferdinando Provesi, 54, (1770 – 1833, aged 63, Italian opera composer), *maestro di cappella* at San Bartolomeo cathedral in Busseto, director of the municipal music school and co-director of the local *Società Filarmonica* (Philharmonic Society). The other director of the Philharmonic Society was Antonio Barezzi, 37, (23 Dec 1787 – 21 July 1867, aged 79.6, a wholesale grocer and distiller, had 3 daughters (the eldest being Margherita), who liked music).

28 Sept 2008, in Piazza Duomo, looking northeast to the southwest façade of Il Duomo di Verona (1120-1187, Cattedrale Santa Maria Matricolare, Romanesque cathedral erected after a powerful earthquake in 1117, which destroyed two Palaeo-Christian churches on the same site), 60 m south of the Adige River. The two storied projecting porch (or protiro), with sculptures, is the work, around 1150, of the sculptor Nicholaus. The portico is supported on the backs of two griffins (legendary creatures with the body, tail, and back legs of a lion; the head and wings of an eagle; and an eagle's talons as their front feet; since the lion was considered the king of the beasts and the eagle the king of birds, the griffins were believed to be particularly powerful and magnificent creatures).

1825 – Verdi, 12, continued his schooling, and began to compose.

1826 – Verdi, 13, continuing until 18, wrote, as he 53 years later stated, many marches, little sinfonia used in church, concertos, variations for pianoforte, serenades, cantatas, church music.

By chance, when he was 13, Verdi was asked to step in as a replacement to play in what became his first public event in his home town Le Roncole; he was an immediate success, mostly playing his own music, to the surprise of many, and receiving strong local recognition.

1827 – 26 March – Verdi was 13.4 when Ludwig von Beethoven died (17 Dec 1770 – 26 March 1827, aged 56 years, 3 months and 9 days).

June – Verdi, 13.6 had graduated with honors from the *Ginnasio,* and was able to focus solely on music under Provesi, 57.

1828 – Verdi, 15, wrote an eight-movement cantata, *I deliri di Saul,* based on a drama by Count Vittorio Alfieri (16 Jan 1749 – 8 Oct 1803, aged 54.7, Italian dramatist and poet, considered the founder of Italian tragedy; Alfieri and his lover (for 25 years (1778 (when he was 29 and she was 26)– 1803)) Louise, the Countess of Albany (20 Sep 1752 – 29 Jan 1824, aged 71.3, the wife from 1772 (when she was 19.6 and he was 51.3) of Charles Edward Stuart (31 Dec 1720 in Rome – 31 Jan 1788 in Rome, aged 67.1, burial: St. Peter's Basilica, Vatican City) the Jacobite claimant to the English and Scottish thrones. Louise was recognized by Jacobites as Queen Louise of England, Scotland, France, and Ireland. After Alfieri's death in 1803, Louise, 51, continued to live in Florence until 1809, when she (57) was summoned to Paris by Napoleon, 40, during France's war with Britain. He asked if she had ever given birth to Charles Edward's child, hoping to find a legal heir who could then be used to cause insurrection in Britain. When she replied "no", the meeting was abruptly terminated. A year later, she (58) was allowed to return to Florence) are buried at the church of Santa Croce at Florence; Alfieri is buried between the tombs of Machiavelli (3 May 1469 – 21 June 1527, aged 58.1, Italian diplomat, politician, historian, philosopher, humanist, and writer of the Renaissance period.) and Michelangelo (6 March 1475 – 18 Feb 1564, aged 88.9, 16 days before 89, an Italian sculptor, painter, architect and poet, one of the greatest artists of all time)). Verdi's cantata was performed in Bergamo (50 km northeast of Milano).

Italy, Vatican, Basilica Papale di San Pietro (1506), an ancient Egyptian obelisk (center right, of red granite, 25.5 m, 41 m total, from Heliopolis, Egypt, 2400 BC, moved by Emperor Augustus in 30 BC to Alexandria, in 37 to Rome, here in 1586).

1829 – Verdi was 16 when Gioachino Rossini, 37, retired, being the most popular opera composer at that time.
Verdi had established himself as a leader of the Philharmonic Society.
In late 1829, Verdi had completed his studies with Provesi, who declared that he had no more to teach him. At the time, Verdi, 16, had been giving singing and piano lessons to Barezzi's daughter Margherita, 15.5.

1830 – Verdi, 17, returned to Busseto, became the town music master and, with the support of Antonio Barezzi, a local merchant and music lover, who had long supported Verdi's musical ambitions in Milan, Verdi gave public performances at Barezzi's home.

1831 – Verdi, 18, and Margherita, 17.5, were unofficially engaged.

1833 – Verdi, 20, went to Milan to continue his studies; he applied unsuccessfully to study at the Conservatory. He took private lessons in counterpoint, while attending operatic performances, as well as concerts of German music.

Barezzi made arrangements for him to become a private pupil of Vincenzo Lavigna, 57, (21 Feb 1776 – 14 Sep 1836, aged 60.5, composer), who had been *maestro concertatore* at Teatro alla Scala (1778, capacity 2,030). Lavigna encouraged Verdi to take out a subscription to La Scala, where he heard Maria Malibran, 25, (24 March 1808 – 23 Sep 1836, aged 28.5, Spanish mezzo-soprano, one of the most famous singers) in operas by Gioachino Rossini, 41, and Vincenzo Bellini, 32. Lavigna introduced Verdi to an amateur choral group, the *Società Filarmonica*, led by Pietro Massini

Verdi's younger sister Giuseppa passed at 17 (1816 – 1833).

Ferdinando Provesi died (1770 – 1833, aged 63, Italian opera composer).

1834 – Verdi, 21, attended the *Società Filarmonica* frequently, and soon found himself functioning as rehearsal director (for Rossini's (42) *La cenerentola,* premiered, with Rossini, 25, as conductor, on 25 Jan 1817 at Teatro Valle in Roma), and continuo player. It was Massini who encouraged him to write his first opera, originally titled *Rocester*, to a libretto by the journalist Antonio Piazza.

Verdi sought to acquire Provesi's former post in Busseto, but without success. However, with Barezzi's help he did obtain the secular post of *maestro di musica*. He taught, gave lessons, and conducted the Philharmonic for several months, before returning to Milan in early 1835.[1]

1835 – July - Verdi obtained his certification from Lavigna in Milano.

23 September - Vincenzo Bellini died (3 November 1801 – 23 September 1835, aged 33.9, Italian opera composer).

Verdi became director of the Busseto School, with a three-year contract.

1836 – 4 May - Verdi, 22.6, after Barezzi invited him 7 years ago to be his daughter Margherita's, 22.1, music teacher, and the two soon fell deeply in love, being unofficially engaged for 5 years, they were married.

14 September - Vincenzo Lavigna died (21 Feb 1776 – 14 Sep 1836, aged 60.5, composer).

23 September - Maria Malibran died at 28.5, after falling from her horse (24 March 1808 – 23 Sep 1836, Spanish mezzo-soprano, one of the most famous singers).

Italy, Venezia, Libreria Sansoviniana (left), Il Campanile (center-left), Palazzo Ducale (right), and a Japanese couple wedding picture.

1837 – 26 March - Verdi, 23.4, and his wife Margherita, 22.9, had their first child Virginia Maria Luigia (26 March 1837 – 12 August 1838, 1 year and 4 months).

Verdi was working on his first opera, and he asked for Massini's assistance to stage his opera in Milan. The La Scala impresario, Bartolomeo Merelli, 43, (19 May 1794 – 10 April 1879, aged 84.9, Italian impresario and librettist, best known as the manager of the La Scala Milan opera house between 1829 and 1850, and for his support for the young Giuseppe Verdi), agreed to put on *Oberto, conte di San Bonifacio* (as the reworked opera was now called, with a libretto rewritten by Temistocle Solera, 22, (25 Dec 1815 – 21 April 1878, aged 62.3, Italian opera composer and librettist).

1838 – 11 July - Verdi, 24.7, and his wife Margherita, 24.2 had their second child Icilio Romano (11 July 1838 – 22 October 1839, 1 year and 3 months).

12 August - their first child Virginia Maria Luigia passed at 1 year and 4 months (26 March 1837 – 12 August 1838).

1839 – 22 October - their second child Icilio Romano passed at 1 year and 3 months (11 July 1838 – 22 October 1839).

29 November - Verdi, 26.1, had the production by Milan's La Scala of his first opera, Oberto, which achieved a respectable 13 additional performances, then Bartolomeo Merelli, La Scala's impresario, offered Verdi a contract for three more works.

1840 – 18 June – Verdi was 26.7 when his wife Margherita died of encephalitis, aged only 26 years 1 month and 14 days. Verdi adored his wife and children, and he was devastated by their untimely deaths.

Verdi was working on his second opera *Un giorno di regno*, melodramma giocoso, a comedy.

5 September – Verdi's *Un giorno di regno* was premiered at the Teatro alla Scala in Milano. It was a failure and only given the one performance. Following its failure, it is claimed Verdi vowed never to compose again, but in his *Sketch* he recounts how Merelli persuaded him to write a new opera. La Scala revived the opera in 2001.

1841 – Verdi, 28, began to work on the music for *Nabuccodonosor*, the libretto of which had originally been rejected by the composer Otto Nicolai, 31, (9 June 1810 – 11 May 1849, aged 38.9, German composer, conductor, and one of the founders of the Vienna Philharmonic).

Autumn – Verdi's completed his opera *Nabuccodonosor*.

1842 – 9 March - Verdi, 28.5 had his opera *Nabuccodonosor* premiered at Teatro alla Scala in Milano, librettist Temistocle Solera, 26.7, based on biblical books, with the famous chorus "Va, pensiero, sull'ali dorate" ("Fly, thought, on golden wings"), and in the role of Abigaille was soprano Giuseppina Strepponi, 26.6, (8 Sep 1815 – 14 Nov 1897, aged 82.2, operatic soprano of great renown). Well received at its first performance, *Nabucco* strengthened Verdi's success until his retirement from the theatre, twenty-nine operas (including some revised and updated versions) later.

Italia, Milano - 30 Sep 2008, in Piazza della Scala (Largo Antonio Ghiringhelli (1906-1979, left), looking northwest to the southeast façade of Teatro alla Scala (3 August 1778, capacity 2,800).

Autumn season - At Nabucco's revival in La Scala, it was given an unprecedented (and later unequalled) total of 57 performances; within three years it had reached (among other venues) Vienna, Lisbon, Barcelona, Berlin, Paris and Hamburg.

The chorus "Va, pensiero" from this opera, and similar choruses in later operas, were much in the spirit of the unification movement, and the composer himself became esteemed as a representative of these ideals.

Verdi settled in Milan, making a number of influential acquaintances. He attended the *Salotto Maffei*, Countess Clara Maffei's, 28, (13 March 1814 – 13 July 1886, aged 72.3, Italian woman of letters and backer of the Risorgimento), salons in Milan, becoming her lifelong friend and correspondent.

Starting this year, a period of hard work for Verdi — with the creation of twenty operas (excluding revisions and translations)—followed over the next sixteen years, culminating in *Un ballo in maschera,* in 1859.

1843 – 11 February – Verdi was 29.3 when his opera I Lombardi alla prima crociata (time of the story: 1096-1097) was premiered at Teatro alla Scala in Milano, librettist Temistocle Solera.

March – Verdi, 29.4 visited Vienna (where Gaetano Donizetti, 45.3, was musical director), to oversee a production of *Nabucco*. The older composer recognized Verdi's talent, and wrote favorably about him.

Verdi, 29.5 travelled on to Parma (30 km southeast of Le Roncole), where the Teatro Regio di Parma was producing *Nabucco* with Strepponi, 27.4, in the cast. For Verdi the performances were a personal triumph in his native region, especially as his father, Carlo, 57, attended the first performance. Verdi remained in Parma for some weeks beyond his intended departure date. This fueled speculation that the delay was due to Verdi's interest in Giuseppina Strepponi (who stated that their relationship began in 1843). Strepponi was in fact known for her amorous relationships (and many illegitimate children, abandoned at orphanages), and her history was a difficult factor in their relationship, until they eventually agreed on marriage.

Nabucco was also performed 25 times at La Fenice in Venezia.

Italy, Venezia - Procuratie Nuove (right), Fermata San Marco (center-right), Giardini Reali (right), Chiesa San Fantin (in the back, near Teatro La Fenice), Capitano di Porto (center), Palazzo Giustinian (center-left), at the east entrance in the Canal Grande.

1844 – 9 March - Verdi was 30.4 when his opera Ernani was premiered at Teatro La Fenice in Venezia, librettist Francesco Maria Piave, 33.8, based on Hernani by Victor Hugo, 42, (26 Feb 1802 – 22 May 1885, aged 83.2, great French poet, novelist, and dramatist).

April – Verdi, 30.5, took on Emanuele Muzio, 22.6, (24 August 1821 – 27 Nov 1890 in Paris, aged 69.2, Italian composer, conductor and vocal teacher. He was a lifelong friend, and the only student of Giuseppe Verdi), as a pupil and assistant. He had known him since about 1828, when they were 15 and 7, as another of Barezzi's protégés.

May – Verdi, 30.6, purchased, near Le Roncole, Il Pulgaro, 62 acres (23 hectares) of farmland with a farmhouse and outbuildings, providing a home for his parents.

3 November – Verdi was 31 when his opera I due Foscari, based on Lord Byron's (22 Jan 1788 in London – 19 April 1824, in Missolonghi, Ottoman Empire, aged 36.2, English nobleman, poet, peer, and politician), play The two Foscari, was premiered at Teatro

Argentina in Rome, librettist Francesco Maria Piave, 34.5, (18 May 1810 – 5 March 1876, aged 65.9, Italian opera librettist, who was born in Murano in the lagoon of Venice, during the brief Napoleonic Kingdom of Italy).

Verdi paid close attention to his financial contracts, making sure he was appropriately remunerated as his popularity increased. He was paid 12,000 lira ($55,000 now) per opera, and this increased to 18,000 lira ($85,000 now), and then more. Verdi bought the Palazzo Cavalli (now known as the Palazzo Orlandi) on the Via Roma, Busseto's main street.

Italy, Venezia - The Doge Francesco Foscari kneeling before the Winged Lion, the symbol of Venice, which holds the book quoting *"Pax Tibi Marce Evangelista Meus"* (Peace to you, Mark, my evangelist).

1845 – 15 February – Verdi was 31.3 when his opera Giovanna d'Arco was premiered at Teatro alla Scala in Milano.

12 August - Verdi was 31.9 when his opera Alzira was premiered at Teatro San Carlo in Napoli, based on Voltaire's (21 Nov 1694 – 30 May 1778, aged 83.5, French writer, historian and philosopher) play *Alzire, ou les Américains*.

1846 – 17 March - Verdi was 32.4 when his opera Attila was premiered at Teatro La Fenice in Venezia, librettists Temistocle Solera and Francesco Maria Piave.

September - After a period of illness Verdi, 32.9, began work on *Macbeth*, and he dedicated the opera to Barezzi, 58.8.

October - Verdi was 33 when Giuseppina Strepponi, 31, because of her vocal deterioration, had to retire from the stage, and she moved to Paris to become a singing teacher. Verdi gave her a love letter, which she treasured very much.

Paris - The north and east sides of l'Arc de Triomphe de l'Étoile, started by Napoleon in 1806, height 50 m, wide 45 m, deep 22 m.

1847 – 14 March - Verdi was 33.4 when his opera Macbeth was premiered at Teatro della Pergola in Firenze, librettists Piave and Andrea Maffei, 49, (1798 – 1885, aged 87, Italian poet, translator and librettist), based on Shakespeare's (23 April 1564 – 23 April 1616, aged 52) play Macbeth.

22 July – Verdi was 33.8 when his opera I masnadieri was premiered, with him as conductor, at Her Majesty's Theatre in

London, librettist Andrea Maffei, based on Friedrich von Schiller's (10 Nov 1759 – 9 May 1805, aged 45.5, German poet, philosopher, physician, historian, and playwright) Die Räuber. Queen Victoria, 28.2, (24 May 1819 – 22 Jan 1901, aged 81.6) and Prince Albert, 27.9 (26 August 1819 – 14 Dec 1861, aged 42.3) attended the first performance, together with the Duke of Wellington, 78.2, (1 May 1769 – 14 Sep 1852, aged 83.3).

Verdi had met in London the nationalist leader Giuseppe Mazzini, who, in 1848, requested Verdi (who complied) to write a patriotic hymn.

27 July - For the next two years, Verdi lived together with Giuseppina in Paris.

26 November - Verdi was 34.1 when his opera Jérusalem was premiered at Salle Le Peletier (The Paris Opéra) in Paris, based on Verdi's I Lombardi alla prima crociata of 1843.

Verdi was awarded the Order of Chevalier of the Legion of Honor.

The west façade of the Church of St Margaret of Antioch (1523, the Anglican parish church of the House of Commons), 20 m northeast of the Westminster Abbey (to the right).

1848 – 11 April - Gaetano Donizetti died (29 November 1797 – 8 April 1848, aged 50.4, Italian composer).

May – Verdi, 34.6, signed a contract for land and houses at Sant'Agata in Busseto, which had once belonged to his family. It was here he built his own house, now known as Villa Verdi.

Verdi was 35 when his opera Nabucco was performed in New York.

25 October – Verdi was 35 when his opera *Il corsaro* from a libretto by Francesco Maria Piave, based on Lord Byron's poem *The Corsair*. The first performance was given at the Teatro Grande in Trieste.

22 Oct 2009, in Piazza Giuseppe Verdi, looking north to Teatro Lirico Giuseppe Verdi (1813-1901).with Stagione sinfonica 2009, which includes Mozart (1756-1791), Haydn (1732-1809), Paganini (1782-1840), von Weber (1786-1826), and Respighi (1879-1936).

Udine - 3 Nov 2009, in Piazza della Liberta, looking east to the statue of Hercules (left), the column (1539) with San Marco's lion (the symbol of Venezia, right), Via Vittorio Veneto (right down).

1849 – 27 January – Verdi was 35.3 when his opera *La battaglia di Legnano* was premiered at Teatro Argentina in Roma, libretto by Salvadore Cammarano, 47.9, (19 March 1801 – 17 July 1852, aged 51.3). It was based on the play *La Bataille de Toulouse* by Joseph Méry, 52, (21 January 1797 – 17 June 1866, aged 69.4, French writer, journalist, novelist, poet, playwright and librettist), later the co-librettist of Verdi's *Don Carlos*.

This was a patriotic opera, which inspired many Italians.

11 May – Verdi was 35.6 when Otto Nicolai died (9 June 1810 – 11 May 1849, aged 38.9, German composer, conductor, and one of the founders of the Vienna Philharmonic).

July - Verdi and Strepponi left Paris because an outbreak of cholera, and went directly to Busseto, where they lived together, which created serious problems.

Verdi worked on his opera Luisa Miller.

8 December – Verdi was 36.2 when his opera Luisa Miller was premiered at Teatro San Carlo in Napoli, librettist Salvadore Cammarano, 48.7, based on the play *Kabale und Liebe* (*Intrigue and Love*) by the German dramatist Friedrich von Schiller.

1850 – Verdi was 37 when his opera Nabucco was performed in Buenos Aires.

16 November - Verdi was 37.1 when his opera Stiffelio was premiered at Teatro Grande in Trieste, Italian libretto by Francesco Maria Piave.

Trieste - 23 Oct 2009, inside Teatro Verdi, commemoration dedicated to Claudio Monteverdi (1567-1643, composer, gambist, singer, and Catholic priest). He wrote 9 books of Madrigali (1587-1643, the ninth book was published posthumously in 1651), 18 operas, but only L'Orfeo (1609), Il ritorno d'Ulisse in patria (1640), L'incoronazione di Poppea (1642), and the famous aria, Lamento, from his second opera L'Arianna (1608), have survived, and sacred music (Vespro della Beata Vergine (1610), Messa in illo tempore (1610), Mass of Thanksgiving (1631), Messa a 4 da Cappela(1641), and others). Monteverdi developed two styles of composition – the heritage of Renaissance polyphony and the new basso continuo technique of the Baroque. He wrote one of the earliest operas, *L'Orfeo that* is the earliest surviving opera still regularly performed.

1851 – January – Verdi was 37.3 when, because of Strepponi, the relations with his parents, who were living for 6.7 years, from May 1844, at his invitation, on his property, were not very good. Verdi was also concerned about the administration of his newly acquired property at Sant'Agata.

11 March - Verdi was 37.4 when one of his greatest masterpieces, Rigoletto, premiered at Teatro La Fenice in Venice. Based on a play by Victor Hugo, 49, (Le roi s'amuse), the libretto by Francesco Maria Piave had to undergo substantial revisions in order to satisfy the epoch's Austrian censorship, and the composer was on the verge of giving it all up a number of times. The opera quickly became a great success.

Italy, Rome (753 BC, one of the oldest continuously occupied cities in Europe, called Roma Aeterna (The Eternal City) and Caput Mundi (Capital of the World)), in Villa Borghese (1630), a monument (1905, by Lucien Pallez, donated by the French Government) to Victor Hugo (1802 – 1885, the greatest French writer (Hernani (1830, inspired opera Ernani (1844) by Giuseppe Verdi (1813-1901)), Notre-Dame de Paris (1831), Le roi s'amuse (1832, inspired opera Rigoletto (1851) by Giuseppe Verdi)), Les Misérables (1862), Les Contemplations, La Légendre des siècles)).

April – Verdi's parents, father Carlo, 66, and mother Luigia, 64, moved from Sant'Agata, and their son Giuseppe, 37.5, found new premises for them, and helped them financially to settle into their new home.

1 May - Verdi and Strepponi moved into Sant'Agata, in his house, Villa Verdi, where he lived for 49.6 years, until his death.

In May Verdi also received an offer for a new opera from Teatro La Fenice in Venezia, which will be *La Traviata*.

June - Verdi's mother Luigia Uttini Verdi passed (1787 – 1851, aged 64).

Verdi began work on *Il trovatore* after the death of his mother, and the fact that this opera focuses on a mother rather than a father is most probably related to her death.

December - Verdi was 38.2 when he decided to go to Paris with Strepponi, where he concluded an agreement with the Opéra to write what became *Les vêpres siciliennes*.

Japan, north-west of the Sendai Station (1887), on Ekimae Dori, the restaurant Rigoletto, named after the famous opera with the same name, by Giuseppe Verdi (1813 – 1901), who wrote 37 operas, Rigoletto being the 17th, with the premiere at Teatro La Fenice, Venezia, on 11 March 1851.

1852 – February – Verdi attended a performance of Alexander Dumas *fils*'s, 27.5, (27 July 1824 – 27 Nov 1895, aged 71 years and 4 months, French author and playwright, best known for *La Dame aux camélias* (*The Lady of the Camellias*), published in 1848) play, *La Dame aux camélias*; Verdi immediately began to compose music for what would later become *La Traviata*.

Milano: 30 Sep 2008, poster for Corpo di Ballo del Teatro alla Scala, the ballet La Dame aux Camélias (1848) by Alexandre Dumas, fils (1824-1895), music by Frédéric Chopin (1810-1849). Much better known: opera La Traviata (1853) by Giuseppe Verdi (1813-1901).

1853 – 19 January - Verdi was 39.2 when one of his greatest masterpieces, Il Trovatore, premiered at Teatro Appolo in Rome, Italian libretto largely written by Salvadore Cammarano, based on the play *El trovador* (1836) by Antonio García Gutiérrez, 39.2, 5 days older than Verdi, (4 October 1813, in Chiclana de la Frontera, Cádiz – 26 August 1884, in Madrid, aged 70.9, Spanish Romantic dramatist).⁾

6 March – Verdi was 39.4 when his opera La Traviata was premiered at Teatro La Fenice in Venice, set to an Italian libretto by Francesco Maria Piave. It was based on Alexandre Dumas, fils' play

La Dame aux camélias, and became the most popular of all operas, placing first in the current Operabase list of most performed operas worldwide.

This opera was Verdi's 16th in the last 11 years.

1855 – 13 June - Verdi was 41.6 when his opera Les vêpres siciliennes, commissioned by the Paris Opéra, and initially given in French, was premiered, set to a French libretto by Eugène Scribe and Charles Duveyrier from their work *Le duc d'Albe*, which was written in 1838 for Donizetti.

1856 – February -Verdi was 42.3 when he relaxed, walking the fields around his house, from sunrise, which he liked to see up and dressed, until sunset, after many years of intense work on his operas.

1857 – 12 March - Verdi was 43.4 when his opera *Simon Boccanegra* was premiered at Teatro La Fenice in Venezia, Italian libretto by Francesco Maria Piave, based on the play *Simón Bocanegra* (1843) by Antonio García Gutiérrez, 43.4.

16 August - Verdi was 43.8 when his opera Aroldo (originally Stiffelio of 1850) was premiered at Teatro Nuovo Comunale in Rimini, Italian libretto by Francesco Maria Piave.

1858 – January – Verdi was 44.2 when he went with Strepponi to Napoli to work with Antonio Somma, 48.4, on the libretto of the opera *Gustave III*, which over a year later would become *Un ballo in maschera*.

1859 – 17 February - Verdi was 45.3 when his opera Un ballo in maschera was premiered at Teatro Apollo in Rome, with text by Antonio Somma, 49.5, (28 August 1809 – 8 August 1864, aged 54.9, Italian playwright). Somma's libretto was itself based on the five act libretto which playwright Eugène Scribe. 67.1, (24 Dec 1791 – 20 Feb 1861, aged 69.1, French dramatist and librettist) had written for Daniel Auber's, 77, (29 Jan 1782 – 12 May 1871, aged 89.3, French composer) 1833 opera, Gustave III, ou Le bal masqué. Scribe wrote about the assassination in 1792 of King Gustav III (24 Jan 1746 – 29 March 1792, aged 46.2, King of Sweden for 21 years:

12 Feb 1771 – 29 March 1792), who was killed as the result of a political conspiracy against him. He was shot while attending a masked ballroom dance, and died 13 days later of his wounds. Because of the censorship, Un ballo in maschera was set in Boston during the colonial era.

March - Arriving in Sant'Agata, Verdi and Strepponi found the nearby city of Piacenza occupied by about 6,000 Austrian troops, who had made it their base, to combat the rise of Italian interest in unification in the Piedmont region. Verdi expressed his strong Italian feelings, and began to take an active interest in Italian politics.

In Naples, and then spreading throughout Italy, the slogan "Viva Verdi" was used as an acronym for *Viva Vittorio Emanuele Re* D'Italia *(Viva Victor Emmanuel (14 March 1820 – 9 Jan 1878, aged 57.9, King of Italy for 16.9 years: 17 March 1861 -9 Jan 1978) King of Italy)*, (who was then king of Sardinia-Piedmont (23 March 1849 – 17 March 1861)).

29 August – Verdi, 45.8, married with Giuseppina Strepponi, 43.9, at Collonges-sous-Salève, a village then part of Piedmont, now in France, elevation 500 m – 1300 m, 6 km south of Geneva.

Verdi was elected as a member of the new provincial council, and was appointed to head a group of five who would meet with King Vittorio Emanuele II, 39, in Torino. They were enthusiastically greeted along the way and in Torino Verdi himself received much of the publicity.

17 October – Verdi, 46, met with the Count of Cavour, 49.2, (10 August 1810 in Torino, French Empire – 6 June 1861, in Torino, Kingdom of Italy, aged 50.9, first Prime Minister of Italy) the architect of the initial stages of Italian unification. Cavour was anxious to convince a man of Verdi's stature that running for political office was essential to strengthening and securing Italy's future.

Italy, Rome (753 BC, one of the oldest continuously occupied cities in Europe, called Roma Aeterna (The Eternal City) and Caput Mundi (Capital of the World)), in Piazza Quirinale, the northeast side of Fountain of Castor (1818), with Obelisco del Quirinale (or Monte Cavallo, 1786, 29 m, from Mausoleum of Augustus (63 BC-14 AD)), and statues of the Dioscuri (Castor and Pollux, twin sons of Zeus and Leda) from the thermal baths of Constantine (272-337), Opus Phidiai on the left.

1860 – Verdi was 47 when hee began to remodel Sant'Agata, which took most of 1860 to complete, and on which he continued to work for the next twenty years.

Verdi declined the office of provincial council member, to which he had been elected *in absentia*.

December - an approach was made from Saint Petersburg's Imperial Theatre of Russia, the offer of 60,000 francs plus all expenses was doubtless a strong incentive. Verdi came up with the idea of adapting the 1835 Spanish play *Don Alvaro o la fuerza del sino* by Angel Saavedra, which became *La forza del destino*, with Piave writing the libretto.

1861 – 3 February – Verdi was 47.2 when he was elected for the town of Borgo San Donnino (Fidenza) to the Parliament of Piedmont-Sardinia in Turin (which from 17 March 1861 became the Parliament of the Kingdom of Italy), but following the death of Cavour in on 6 June 1861, which deeply distressed him, he scarcely attended.

17 March - Verdi was 47.3 when The Kingdom of Italy was officially founded, with King Vittorio Emanuele II.

6 June - the Count of Cavour died (10 August 1810 in Torino, French Empire – 6 June 1861, in Torino, Kingdom of Italy, aged 50.9, first Prime Minister of Italy).

December - Verdi and his wife arrived in St. Petersburg (2,200 km northeast of Milano), Russia, for the premiere of *La forza del destino*, but casting problems meant that it had to be postponed for almost one year.

1862 – 71 years after Mozart's passing, Ludwig von Köchel, 62, (14 Jan 1800 – 3 June 1877, aged 77.4, Austrian musicologist, writer, composer, botanist and publisher) published the Köchel catalogue, a chronological and thematic register of the works of Mozart. This catalogue was the first on such a scale, and with such a level of scholarship behind it; it has since undergone revisions. Mozart's works are often referred to by their K-numbers (*K* for *Köchel*); for example, the "Jupiter" symphony, *Symphony No. 41* K. 551.

24 February – Verdi, 48.2, returned via Paris from Russia, and met two young Italian writers, Arrigo Boito, 20, (24 February 1842– 10 June 1918, aged 76.3, Italian poet, journalist, novelist, librettist and composer) and Franco Faccio, 21.9, (8 March 1840 in Verona – 21 July 1891 in Monza, aged 51.3, Italian composer, conductor, between 1871 and 1889 music director of the Teatro alla Scala opera house, where he became known as a conductor of Verdi's music at La Scala, then in different parts of Italy, and abroad). Verdi had been invited to write a piece of music for the 1862 International Exhibition in London, and charged Boito with writing a text, which became the *Inno delle nazioni*.

24 May – Verdi was 48.6 when his cantata *Inno delle nazioni* was performed at Her Majesty's Theatre in London, text by Arrigo Boito.

The west façade and entrance of Westminster Abbey (960, 1517, Collegiate Church of St Peter at Westminster, Anglican abbey with daily services and coronations since 1066, tower height 69 m).

22 November - Verdi was 49.1 when his opera La forza del destino, commissioned by the Imperial Theatre of Saint Petersburg for 1861, but performed now. The libretto was written by Francesco

Maria Piave, based on a Spanish drama, Don Álvaro o la fuerza del sino (1835), by Ángel de Saavedra, Duke of Rivas, with a scene adapted from Friedrich Schiller's Wallensteins Lager. It was first performed in the Bolshoi Kamenny Theatre of St. Petersburg, Russia. Verdi received the Order of St. Stanislaus.

1864 – 8 August - Verdi was 50.9 when his librettist Antonio Somma died (28 August 1809 – 8 August 1864, aged 54.9, Italian playwright).

1865 – 21 April - Verdi was 51.5 when his revised version of Macbeth was premiered in French at Théâtre Lyrique in Paris, libretto by Francesco Maria Piave, and additions by Andrea Maffei.

1866 – Fall - Verdi, 53, with his wife spent late of this year and much of the next year in Paris.

Paris - A sculpture with musicians on the right side of the left outer bay on the façade of l'Opéra de Paris (1875), one of the most famous opera house in the world, and a prestigious symbol of Paris. In interior, the ceiling area, which surrounds the chandelier, contains a new 1964 painting by Marc Chagall, which was installed on a removable frame over the original, and depicts scenes from operas by 14 composers, including, Mozart, Bizet, Verdi and Beethoven.

1867 – 11 March - Verdi was 53.4 when his opera Don Carlos, commissioned by the Paris Opéra, and initially given in French, was premiered at Salle Le Peletier (Paris Opéra), libretto by Joseph Méry and Camille du Locle, based on the dramatic play *Don Carlos, Infant von Spanien* by Friedrich Schiller.

After seeing Don Carlos, French composer Georges Bizet, 28.4, (25 Oct 1838 – 3 June 1875, aged 36.7, composer of Carmen, which became, together with Verdi's La Traviata, the most popular and frequently performed works in the entire opera repertoire) commented that Verdi is changing style, and is no longer pure Italian.

21 July - Antonio Barezzi died (23 Dec 1787 – 21 July 1867, aged 79.6, a wholesale grocer and distiller in Busseto, who liked music, and helped young Verdi very much).

Verdi's father Carlo Giuseppe Verdi passed (1785 – 1867, aged 82).

Verdi, 54, and Giuseppina, 52, decided to adopt the daughter of a cousin of Verdi (and father Carlo's great-niece, and granddaughter of Verdi's uncle) Maria Cristina Filomena Verdi (14 Nov. 1859 in Le Roncole, Parma – 1936 in Busseto, aged 77), then eight years old, as their own child. She was to marry at 19, in 1878, the son of Verdi's friend and lawyer Angelo Carrara, and her family became eventually the heirs of Verdi's estate.

1868 – 13 November - Verdi was 55.1 when Gioachino Rossini passed (29 February 1792 – 13 November 1868, aged 76.7, Italian composer who wrote 39 operas, as well as some sacred music, songs, chamber music, and piano pieces; he was a precocious composer of operas, and he made his debut at age 18).

1869 – Verdi, 56, had been asked to compose a section for a requiem mass in memory of Gioachino Rossini, who passed last year. He compiled and completed the requiem, but its performance was abandoned (and its premiere did not take place until 1988).[1]

1871 – 24 December - Verdi, 58.1, had his opera Aida premiered at Cairo's (2,500 km southeast of Milano) Khedivial Opera House, in Egypt. Verdi did not attend the premiere in Cairo.

Aida was commissioned by the Egyptian government for the opera house built by the Khedive Isma'il Pasha to celebrate the opening of the Suez Canal in 1869. The opera house actually opened with a production of *Rigoletto*. The prose libretto in French by Camille du Locle, based on a scenario by the Egyptologist Auguste Mariette, was transformed to Italian verse by Antonio Ghislanzoni. Verdi was offered the beautiful sum of 150,000 francs for the opera (about $2 M now).

Japan, north-west of the Sendai Station (1887), on Ekimae Dori, the restaurant Rigoletto, named after the famous opera with the same name, by Giuseppe Verdi (1813 – 1901), who wrote 37 operas, Rigoletto being the 17th, with the premiere at Teatro La Fenice, Venezia, on 11 March 1851.

1872 – 8 February - Verdi, 58.3, had his opera Aida performed at Teatro Alla Scala in Milano, where he was heavily involved at every stage. In the role of Aida was Teresa Stolz, 37.6 (2 June 1834 in Bohemia – 23 August 1902 in Milano, aged 68.2, Bohemian soprano, long resident in Italy, who was associated with significant premieres of the works of Giuseppe Verdi, and she was very close to him), who had sung in La Scala productions from 1865 onwards.

Milano - 30 Sep 2008, in Piazza della Scala (Largo Antonio Ghiringhelli (1906-1979, left), looking northwest to the southeast corner of Teatro alla Scala (right, 3 Aug. 1778), and the Opera Museum (left)

Verdi spent much of this year and next year supervising the Italian productions of *Aida* at Milan, Parma and Naples, effectively acting as producer, and demanding high standards and adequate rehearsal time. During the rehearsals for the Naples production he wrote his string quartet, the only chamber music by him to survive.

1874 – 22 May - Verdi, 60.6, reworked his "Libera Me" section of the Rossini Requiem, and made it a part of his Requiem Mass, honoring the famous novelist and poet Alessandro Manzoni, who had died in 1873. The complete Requiem was first performed at the cathedral in Milan on this day, with Teresa Stolz, 39.9.

Verdi, 61, was appointed a member of the Italian Senate, but did not participate in its activities.

1875 – Verdi was 62 when his Requiem, with Stolz, 41.3, was performed, under Verdi's direction, at the Royal Albert Hall in London, and then in Paris and Vienna.

London - The Royal Albert Hall (1867-1871, 2004)– an Italian style concert hall on Kensington Gore, on the northern edge of South Kensington, capacity 5,272 seats, 41 m height, named after Prince Consort Albert (1819 (in Germany)-1861), husband (1840-1861) of Queen Victoria (1819-1901, Queen 1837-1901, had 9 children), Chancellor of the University of Cambridge from 1847. In July 1871, French composer Camille Saint-Saëns (1835-1921) performed *Church Scene* from the Faust, by Charles Gounod (1818-1893).

1876 – 5 March – Verdi was 62.4 when his librettist Francesco Maria Piave died (18 May 1810 – 5 March 1876, aged 65.9, Italian opera librettist, who was born in Murano in the lagoon of Venice, during the brief Napoleonic Kingdom of Italy).

Verdi was 63 when his Requiem, with Stolz, 42.3, was performed, under Verdi's direction, in Köln, Germany.

Italy, Murano (Venezia) - A beautiful Murano glass sculpture in Murano Square. Murano's glassmakers created crystalline glass, enameled glass (smalto), glass with threads of gold (aventurine), and multicolored glass.

1878 – 21 April – Verdi was 64.5 when Temistocle Solera died (25 Dec 1815 – 21 April 1878, aged 62.3, Italian opera composer and librettist).

1879 – Verdi, 66, dictated to the publisher Giulio Ricordi, 39, (19 Dec 1840 – 6 June 1912, aged 71.5, an Italian editor and musician, who joined the family firm, the Casa Ricordi music publishing house, in 1863) the *Autobiographical Sketch*.

10 April - Bartolomeo Merelli died (19 May 1794 – 10 April 1879, aged 84.9, Italian impresario and librettist, best known as the manager of the La Scala Milan opera house between 1829 and 1850, and for his support for the young Giuseppe Verdi).

Verdi began work on *Otello*, which Arrigo Boito, 37, (24 February 1842– 10 June 1918, aged 76.3, Italian poet, journalist, novelist, librettist and composer) (recommended by Ricordi, 39) had proposed to him privately. The composition was delayed by a revision of *Simon Boccanegra,* which Verdi undertook with Boito, produced in 1881, and a revision of *Don Carlos*.

1880 – 22 March - Verdi, 66.4, had his opera Aida performed at Palais Garnier, Paris, where he was the conductor.

Verdi was 67 when his house, Villa Verdi, in which he was living for 29 years, from 1851, was completed.

Paris - L'Opéra de Paris (or L'Académie Nationale de Musique, or l'Opéra Garnier, or Le Palais Garnier, or L'Opéra), a 1,979-seat opera house, built from 1861 to 1875, now mainly used for ballet.

1881 – 24 March - Verdi was 67.4 when the second version of his opera *Simon Boccanegra* was premiered at Teatro La Scala in Milano, Italian libretto by Arrigo Boito, 39.1, (24 February 1842– 10 June 1918, aged 76.3, an Italian poet, journalist, novelist, librettist and composer), based on the play *Simón Bocanegra* (1843) by Antonio García Gutiérrez, 67.4.

1885 – 22 May – Verdi was 71.6 when Victor Hugo died (26 Feb 1802 – 22 May 1885, aged 83.2, great French poet, novelist, and dramatist).

Paris - A copy (made in 1964) of the sculpture "The Dance" (1868 – 1869, 4.2 m by 3 m, with a highly animated central male dancer, surrounded by six dancing women (the original is now in the Musée d'Orsay)) by Jean-Baptiste Carpeaux (1827 – 1875, he closely studied the sculpture of Michelangelo (1475 – 1564) in Rome; Garnier commissioned Carpeaux in 1865), on the left side of the right outer bay on the façade of l'Opéra de Paris (1875).

1886 – 13 July – Verdi was 72.7 when Countess Clara Maffei's died (13 March 1814 – 13 July 1886, aged 72.3, Italian woman of letters and backer of the Risorgimento).

25 June – Aida was presented in Rio de Janeiro, Brazil, with a locally hired conductor, who was in a two-month escalating conflict with the performers, due to his rather poor command of the work, to the point that the singers went on strike, and forced the company's general manager to seek a substitute conductor. Two other conductors tried unsuccessfully to finish Aida. In desperation, the singers suggested the name of their assistant Chorus Master, who knew the whole opera from memory – Arturo Toscanini, 19.2, (25 March 1867 – 16 Jan 1957, aged 89.8, the greatest Italian conductor, Music Director at La Scala: 1898 – 1908 and 1921 - 1929). Although he had no conducting experience, Toscanini was eventually persuaded by the musicians to take up the baton at 9:15 PM, and led a performance of the two-and-a-half hour opera, completely from memory. The public was taken by surprise, at first by the youth and sheer aplomb of this unknown conductor, then by his solid mastery. The result was astounding acclaim. For the rest of that season, Toscanini conducted eighteen operas, all with absolute success. Thus began his career as a conductor, at age 19.2.

1887 – 8 December - Verdi, 74.2, had the premiere at Teatro Alla Scala in Milan of his opera Otello, based on William Shakespeare's play, with a libretto written by the younger composer of Mefistofele, Arrigo Boito, 45.8. Arturo Toscanini, 20.7, participated as cellist in this world premiere of Verdi's Otello.

Italia - 23 October 2009, Trieste (177 BC part of the Roman Republic), from Passo Fausto Pecorari, in Piazza San Giovanni, looking southeast to the statue of Giuseppe Verdi (1813-1901), and buildings on Via Giacinto Gallina (left) and Via delle Torri (right).

1888 – Verdi, 75, had his requiem in memory of Gioachino Rossini, composed in 1869, premiered after 19 years.

1889 – July - Verdi, 75.7, received from Boito, 47.4, the draft libretto for Falstaff, after Verdi had just read Shakespeare's play *The Merry Wives of Windsor*. Boito began work some time ago on this libretto, based on *The Merry Wives of Windsor,* with additional material taken from *Henry IV, Part 1* and *Part 2*. Verdi: responded: "Benissimo! Benissimo!", and began working on Falstaff. Boito also informed Verdi about Toscanini's (22.4) ability to interpret Verdi's scores.

1890 – 27 November –Verdi was 77.1 when Emanuele Muzio died (24 August 1821 – 27 Nov 1890 in Paris, aged 69.2, Italian composer, conductor and vocal teacher. He was a lifelong friend, and the only student of Giuseppe Verdi).

1893 – 9 February - Verdi, 79.3, had his last of his 28 operas, Falstaff, premiered at Teatro Alla Scala in Milano, Boito, 50.9, wrote the libretto, based on Shakespeare's *The Merry Wives of*

Windsor, with additional material taken from *Henry IV, Part 1* and *Part 2.*

For the first night, official ticket prices were thirty times higher than usual. Royalty, aristocracy, critics, and leading figures from the arts all over Europe were present. The performance was a huge success; numbers were encored, and at the end the applause for Verdi and the cast lasted an hour. That was followed by a tumultuous welcome when the composer, his wife and Boito arrived at the Grand Hotel et de Milan (400 m northeast of La Scala, on Via Manzoni, 29, opened 30 years before, in 1863).

May - Verdi, 79.6, had his opera Falstaff presented at Teatro Costanzi in Roma.

In Roma, crowds of well-wishers at the railway station initially forced Verdi to take refuge in a toolshed. He witnessed the performance from the Royal Box, at the side of King Umberto I, 48.9, (14 March 1844, in Torino, Kingdom of Sardinia – 29 July 1900 in Monza, Kingdom of Italy, aged 56.3, King of Italy for 22.5 years: 9 Jan 1878 – 29 July 1900), and the Queen Margherita di Savoia, 41.3, (20 Nov 1851 in Torino, Kingdom of Sardinia – 4 Jan 1926 in Bordighera, Italia, aged 74.1).

Italy, Rome (753 BC), Piazza di Monte Citorio, Camera dei Deputati (back), from Via della Guglia the view of the Obelisk of Montecitorio (or Solare, 21.79 m, 33.97 m with base and globe, moved here in 1789): an ancient Egyptian red granite obelisk of Psammetichus II (595-589 BC) from Heliopolis, brought to Rome with the Flaminian obelisk in 10 BC by the Roman Emperor Augustus (63 BC – 14 AD) to be used as the gnomon (the part of a sundial that casts the shadow) of the Solarium (or Horologium) Augusti (10 BC, functioned as a giant Solar clock, built by the mathematician Facondius Novus (circa 50 BC – 15 AD).

1894 – Verdi, 81, published a song for the benefit of earthquake victims in Sicily.

1895 – Verdi, 82, started planning, building and endowing a rest-home for retired musicians in Milan, the Casa di Riposo per Musicisti, and building a hospital at Villanova sull'Arda, close to Busseto.

1897 – 21 August - Verdi, 83.9, completed his last composition, a setting of the traditional Latin text Stabat Mater. This was the last of four sacred works that Verdi composed, Quattro Pezzi Sacri, which are often performed together or separately.
14 November - Verdi was 84.1 when his wife Giuseppina passed (8 Sep 1815 – 14 Nov 1897, aged 82.2, operatic soprano of great renown).
Teresa Stolz, 63.4, remained a companion of Verdi until his death.

1898 – 7 April - Verdi, 84.5, had the first performance of the Quattro Pezzi Sacri at the Grande Opéra, Paris. The four works are: Ave Maria for mixed chorus; Stabat Mater for mixed chorus and orchestra; Laudi alla Vergine Maria for female chorus; and Te Deum for double chorus and orchestra.
Arturo Toscanini, 31, consulted Verdi personally about Verdi's *Te Deum*.

Paris - A sculpture with actors on the left side of the left outer bay on the façade of l'Opéra de Paris (1875), one of the most famous opera house in the world, and a prestigious symbol of Paris. In interior, the Opéra's Auditorium seats almost 2,000 people. Four tiers of balconies surround the ground floor, ending in elaborate forward boxes to the left and right of the stage, with their sculptured caryatids.

1900 – 29 July – Verdi was 86.8 when King Umberto I died (14 March 1844, in Torino, Kingdom of Sardinia – 29 July 1900 in Monza, Kingdom of Italy, aged 56.3, King of Italy for 22.5 years: 9 Jan 1878 – 29 July 1900).

Verdi he was deeply saddened by the death of King Umberto I, whom he met in Roma 7 years before, and sketched a setting of a poem in his memory, but was unable to complete it.

1901 – 21 January – Verdi, 87.2, had a stroke, while staying at the Grand Hotel et de Milan. He gradually grew feebler over the next days, during which Teresa Stolz, 66.5, cared for him

27 January – Verdi died at the age of 87 years, 3 months and 18 days, while staying at the Grand Hotel et de Milan, six days after the stroke.

Verdi was initially buried in Milan's Cimitero Monumental.

February - A month later, his body was moved to the crypt of the Casa di Riposo. On this occasion, "Va, pensiero" from *Nabucco* was conducted by Arturo Toscanini, 33.9, with a chorus of 820 singers. A huge crowd was in attendance, estimated at 300,000. Arturo Toscanini conducted the vast forces of combined orchestras and choirs, composed of musicians from throughout Italy, at the state funeral for Verdi in Milan. To date, it remains the largest public assembly of any event in the history of Italy.

Verdi came to lead the Italian opera scene after the era of Gioachino Rossini, Gaetano Donizetti, and Vincenzo Bellini, whose works significantly influenced him. By his 30s, he had become one of the pre-eminent opera composers in history.

1902 – 14 July – The original Campanile della Basilica di San Marco (1156 – 1173, last restored in 1514), in Venezia, collapsed.

Italy, Venezia - Libreria Sansoviniana (left), La Loggetta (center-left down), Il Campanile (center), and Procuratie Nuove (right). Il Campanile della Basilica di San Marco (1156 – 1173, last restored in 1514), rebuilt in 1912 *com'era, dov'era* (as it was, where it was) after the collapse of the original campanile on 14 July 1902. Adjacent to the Campanile, facing towards the Basilica, is the graceful small building known as La Loggetta, built by Sansovino in 1537 - 1546.

1926 – Over 420 of Vivaldi's compositions thought lost were discovered in a monastery in Piedmont, Italy.

1939 – Due to the efforts of Alfredo Casella, 56, (25 July 1883 – 5 March 1947, aged 63.6, Italian composer, pianist and conductor), some of these compositions were performed at a Vivaldi Week, marking the start of the appreciation of his works in the 20th century. Since 1950, Vivaldi's compositions have enjoyed wide success. A composition by Vivaldi is identified by RV number, which refers to its place in the "Ryom-Verzeichnis" or "Répertoire des oeuvres d'Antonio Vivaldi", a catalog created in the 20th century by the musicologist Peter Ryom (born 31 May 1937 in Copenhagen, Danish musicologist).

2003 – Recent rediscoveries of works by Vivaldi: two psalm settings of *Nisi Dominus* (RV 803, in eight movements).

2005 – *Dixit Dominus* (RV 807, in eleven movements).

2006 – Vivaldi's 1730 opera *Argippo* (RV 697), which had been considered lost, was rediscovered by the harpsichordist and conductor Ondřej Macek.

2008 – 3 May - Ondřej Macek and his Hofmusici orchestra performed Vivaldi's opera *Argippo* (RV 697) at Prague Castle — its first performance in 278 years, since 1730.

2013 – 10 October - the bicentenary of Verdi's birth was widely celebrated in broadcasts and performances.

Italy, Venezia - This ponte is for getting into a gondola, and is situated at the south end of La Piazzetta, the south part of Piazza San Marco. On the center-left back, Isola San Giorgio Maggiore can be seen, with la Chiesa di San Giorgio Maggiore and its Campanile. On the right the Queen Elizabeth cruise ship is leaving Venezia.

www.ingramcontent.com/pod-product-compliance
Lightning Source LLC
Chambersburg PA
CBHW041613220426
43670CB00001B/8